TRY BEING HUMAN

TRY BEING HUMAN

ALEC FORBES
MA DM (Oxon) FRCP (Lond)

LANGDON BOOKS
The Old Laundry, Langdon, Wembury, Plymouth

First printed 1973
Second Impression 1973

ISBN 0 903658 01 1 (Paper Edn)
ISBN 0 903658 00 3 (Cloth Edn)

Printed in Great Britain
by Latimer Trend & Company Ltd
Plymouth

1

Watching One's Mind

FROM time to time most people wonder if their opinions are right, and whether the actions they have taken are for the best. Some are so dogged by uncertainty over all aspects of their lives that they worry and get depressed. This applies to as many of those who are successful, as those who are not. Some people avoid this suffering by assuming a false confidence, and force their opinions on others. This defence reduces their adaptability—so they tend to become specialists—experts in a narrow field where no one can contradict them, or, feel they have to win—so they are obstinate and assertive, and when they lose, or can't have their way, often become violent and depressed, and may even come into conflict with their neighbours, the law, or society. Some go to such extremes they may be classed as insane or shut up in gaol. So everyone has a problem whether he is aware of it or not. Most people have dozens. This book is written both for the person who knows he has difficulties in coping with life, and the person who believes he has none.

Do you feel anxiety, depression, tension or emotional stress? These are feelings we all should understand, and questions each of us could answer. But are you aware of your internal mental processes as well as your external activities? And do you take responsibility for them both? These are questions fewer of us could answer, and many have never considered. There is a connection between these two groups of questions. External activities are actions we all engage in such as: recreations, feeding and clothing ourselves, earning a living, relating to other people, marrying, making a home, and rearing a family. In other words external activity is behaviour. It can be seen, recorded, and even measured. Equally we also engage in inner mental activity. We experience fear, joy, despair, depression, love, anger, envy, suspicion. We have ideas, and think about our feelings. There is a vast range of mentation that can take place without any corresponding behaviour being observed. In animals, in uninhibited people, and in simple situations, there is a much more direct relationship between the inner mental activity and behaviour, so some study behaviour, as it can be measured and recorded by an observer. They think this is all that is required to elucidate human problems because it is impossible to record mental activity in the same direct way. Others think differently, and study the inner activity. They have devised various tests, usually in the form of a questionnaire, since the description by a subject of his mental processes is very unreliable. But these only show the ways a person may react in certain situations. This is useful in finding out what people suit which jobs. But the tests impose their own limitations on the individual, and interfere with his mental activity, so though the results they give may be statistically highly significant, they present a false picture, as well as only a general prediction of how an individual may react. They never show the whole state as it happens. The importance of the inner activity is that it occurs before the behaviour, and is what determines it. Moreover, a complicated animal like man can be taught to inhibit his outer behaviour, and not act directly in accordance with his mentation. For instance, a couple may pass by each other with downcast eyes while experiencing strong sex desire for each other, because they have learnt it is wrong to do otherwise. A soldier can be taught to kill, and be killed, in spite of being terrified. He may even get so brutalised that he enjoys it. Many a boring host has been thanked for a delightful evening. These are simple examples. Human beings are very complex and the rest of this book is an attempt to explain how the human mind works, and muddles itself up, as well as how to modify it by changing its habits.

But given that studying behaviour only is incomplete, and does not help the individual to understand why he behaves that way, and that personality tests just reveal trends, and predict behaviour, but are not any use to an individual in practically dealing with his problems, though they may tell him what some of them are, how is a human being going to begin taking responsibility for, and starting to alter, the feelings and thoughts which distress him? Failure to achieve this leads to drifting through life; one may be lucky to come through unscathed, but most driftwood gets badly knocked about, and some is ground to bits.

First of all it is necessary to learn how to observe inner mental activity. Some people will know how to do this without being taught, but may not be aware of having this ability until it is put to them in these words. Many people only perceive their outer lives, and regard the disturbances and moods that arise from their inner lives, only as external problems. They have not seen that they have an inner mind. Therefore it is necessary to introduce here an exercise which will demonstrate that everyone has an inner life, and show how to observe it. This is real, practical, psychology. Reading about mental processes doesn't get anyone, anywhere. It is only personal observation that produces changes in the mind, but because you think you understand, do not avoid this exercise. Thinking is misleading—it is like playing with a kaleidoscope. New patterns based on the coloured pieces of glass emerge—but nothing new enters. Practice is essential—real mental activity is understanding. It is not putting ideas into words or pictures, to use for memory and imagination. In addition, there is a lot more to be learnt from this exercise which will be made clear later, so everyone should do it with full attention and intent to understand what they can learn from doing it.

The Watch Exercise

Find a spot where you will not be interrupted for ten minutes. Take a watch with a second hand, and keep looking at it. Try to think of nothing except the second hand moving in tiny jerks round its dial. Aim at an intense awareness of the tip of the tiny strip of metal as it moves. As you do this, your attention will be distracted from your aim by noises, movements, sensations from the body, thoughts and feelings that come into your mind. At each distraction, remember your aim, and bring your attention back to the tip of the second hand. But remember what distracted you. Nobody can do this for more than a few minutes without an intrusion of an idea, a mental image, a thought, or a sensation from the body such as an itch or tension. If one is in a noisy place, the distractions will begin at once, and the task can be harder. It is better to start in a quiet spot, where one will be undisturbed. Doing the exercise turns one's attention both outwards and inwards. The attention is focused down on to a tiny moving point as well as expanded to take in abstractions, ideas, thoughts and feelings, which cannot be perceived through the physical senses. Doing this exercise rightly enlarges a person's attention so that many more impressions than usual are taken in.

In fact, the term 'Watch' Exercise is a play on words. You use a watch to watch what is going on in your mind.

After about five minutes, stop and take stock of the observations you have made. Of the people who have made no observations a few may be liars. Suspicious, secretive, or frightened, they may not want to reveal anything of themselves to another. Or they may be one of those people who obtain satisfaction from making others fail. Whatever your reaction is, try to acknowledge it. The majority of people who have made no observations are genuine in their response. They are movers rather than thinkers or feelers, and they have a strong power of concentration. They are mostly manual workers. Often, it only takes a few questions such as 'Did you want to laugh?'; 'Did you think you were being hypnotized?'; 'Did you wonder how long it was going on for?'; 'Did you think of the children, your work, your wife, etc.?'. For them to realize that they have had thoughts, or feelings which interrupted the 'Watch' Exercise. If no observations are made, the exercise should be repeated after an interval in which a short spell of another activity, or some deep breaths of fresh air out of doors, are undertaken. It should be borne in mind that the main part of the exercise is not to concentrate on the tip of the second hand of the watch, but to make the observations of what comes into the mind during the 'watching'. In fact, it is not necessary to use a watch at all. Imagining a blank screen, trying to think of nothing else, and then observing what distracts one from doing this, can be used instead. But this is too abstract for some people to do, and encourages others to use their overdeveloped imagination too much. So a practical sense based activity such as concentrating on the tip of the second hand of a watch is best, to focus the attention, while it is also being expanded to take in mental activity.

Many people mention noises, movements, or sensations as things that came into their minds during the exercise. They do not notice any thoughts or feelings. This may be because they are the same as the type of person just mentioned, or because they do not have many thoughts and feelings going on at the time the exercise was done. If so, the exercise should be repeated, and, if there is still no response, then, after a period of activity especially when one is feeling upset—for example, after an argument.

The above has been written to help those who have initial difficulties to use the exercise correctly. If you have them, stop here and go on doing the exercise until you have genuinely observed a thought or a feeling come into your mind and distract your attention from the set task of concentrating on the tip of the second hand of the watch. If you are good at learning from books, do not just read on, saying, 'Yes, quite simple, I see what is meant.' Stop here, too. Really do this exercise practically until you, too, have experienced observation of your thoughts and feelings. People who think and imagine too much, run away from reality more than they realize.

Now, the majority of people, about two-thirds, on their first performance of this 'Watch' exercise, make a genuine observation of a distracting thought or feeling. The next step is to do the 'Watch' exercise at least once a day. It takes less than five minutes. This is done in order to learn what it feels like to be attentive to your mental activity. This can be called self-observation, or being in attention. You cannot learn anything or take in anything new, without being in this state. Young people, especially students, will recognize that they have been in this state before. Other people may have to learn to experience it again. Whoever you are, get familiar with it before you get much older, if you really want to change yourself. Then you can use it as much as possible—all the time if you can—to help you deal with your problems and your life.

The method of working upon your mind described in this book is effective. It works with one-third of those who try to use it. They lose their symptoms, anxiety, or depression, whatever their problem is. They still become depressed and anxious as before, but having found out how to transform and deal with their reactions, need no longer remain in those states. Of the two-thirds who get no benefit, one-third understand but cannot overcome their own inertia or laziness, so they do not sustain practical work on themselves long enough to produce a change; and one-third have personalities closed to the functions of the mind. Their interest is confined to material things. Some, in fact many, are intelligent people, but intelligence has nothing to do with understanding. By understanding is meant an ability to appreciate the motives that govern behaviour—to have enough humanity to put oneself in another's place, and see his point of view. Human understanding is not the ability to solve puzzles, do intelligence tests, and learn what is taught in school easily. It is worth pondering over this a bit. Some people who are poorly developed academically have great understanding, and may be inclined to rate their abilities too low. Some who have academic facility, may so lack understanding, that they brush these ideas aside as being too simple. Human intelligence and understanding really are two entirely different things.

Some people of a scientific turn of mind cannot accept anything unless it can be proved by a statistical analysis. The problem for them is that in biological analysis, especially of something so changeable and vague as symptoms and emotional states, any treatment which only helps a third of the people that try it cannot be proved to work by statistical methods. But besides statistics, there is proof by individual experience. If something has worked for you, you know it has. When it works again and again, you do not need anything else to convince you. This is proof by experience. It is impossible to prove to someone that water is cold and wet if he will not jump into it and has not got a thermometer. It is the same with people. In Human relations you have to open yourself to the other person, and join with them in mutual understanding. Sometimes it can be like holding your hand out in the dark to an animal. It may be bitten, but the risk must be taken, otherwise you will never make contact. Experience in understanding yourself is impossible unless you are willing enough, and fearless enough to act. It is in your power, alone, to make what you will of your life, and your way of taking life.

2

Trapped in a Cage

WHY am I here? Where am I going? These are questions asked when a person's sense of individuality has emerged from the mist of childhood. An answer cannot be made then, because in youth there is no experience and little understanding. Nor do our apparently omniscient elders give a satisfactory response to our questions. Only a few individuals are tenacious enough to go on enquiring. Most of these become confused by the discordant responses, and either accept an explanation which suits their fancy, or give up and drift, others get it beaten out of them. Those who persist find that the answer is within themselves. How in the midst of the incredible, wonderful diversity of human beings, each always a unique individual, can people yet be the same underneath? What is the basic stuff which allows such an unlimited variability? These questions can only be answered through observing and digesting one's thoughts, one's feelings, one's ideas, and one's patterns of behaviour. Other people's explanations are mostly second-hand and may even be third- or fourth-hand, and are usually written in such unintelligible jargon that further education and a devoted interest are required to understand them. But, luckily, the quest can start with oneself. No-one can understand anyone else unless he has understood and accepted the same in himself—so Psychology is for everyone—everyone, that is, who wants to try to understand himself.

Man's fundamental difference from other animals is not that he can think and they cannot, but that he is more conscious of what is going on in his mind. He can have what is called insight. This allows him to use his mental apparatus much more effectively than the other animals, to elaborate its responses and to adapt rapidly to changing situations by modifying his reactions to them. Insight functions as a sixth sense. It allows a man to look at himself impersonally, so that he can be the spectator of his inner life of thoughts and feelings, just as he is the spectator of the external events of his life. Like the other senses, the information supplied by it is always available, but may be ignored. Its perceptions can be widened and sharpened by practice, just as they can be lost by never being used, as with any other sense. It may be naturally well developed in one individual, or feeble in another. If the faculty of insight is used, observation of one's reactions is possible, and this permits their change in those who wish it, for, only if people perceive why and how they react as they do, can their habits be altered. This allows a far wider range of responses to external events than is possible to an animal. Those in whom the faculty is poorly developed or lost, are unable to change themselves. Their reactions to external events are limited, so that if these change too much they produce inappropriate responses. This can be observed in the elderly who tend to regret that things are not as they were, unable to perceive that this can never be, and it is they who are not as they should be. It also occurs in the not-so-old, who wonder why their children behave differently from the way they did at the same age. The same mechanism of inappropriate responses occurs in some forms of mental disturbance. People with a limited range of responses break down when faced with stressful new situations from which they cannot escape, such as puberty, earning a living, living alone, or the death of relatives. These are common situations which preceed a breakdown of health—mental or physical, or both mental and physical.

Everyone's mind is divided into a part which is known—there are pet likes and aversions, fixed attitudes and ways of taking the familiar events of life. But there is also an unknown side—unpleasant events or things of which we are ashamed, rapidly fade from memory, but the adaptations made to them and the compensations to prevent feeling the same again, go on operating unperceived. We sometimes find ourselves behaving in an unusual way to a familiar event. Sometimes we make unexpected mistakes. We are divided into conscious and unconscious sides. We are also made up of several different people. We behave in one way when with our parents, in another when with our children or schoolfriends of the same sex, with those in authority over us, from those whom it is our task to direct, from our wives and husbands, compared with others of the opposite sex. The different facets of our personality are numerous. Those we know enough about to be able to recognize, we have the chance of managing and even retraining. Those we do not know, rule us because we do not know them. They form part of our unconscious minds.

If we want to change a habit, for example to give up smoking, we have to use the sixth sense and watch the part of us that wants to smoke all the time. If we do this carefully, we learn a lot. This smoker in ourselves is easily upset. If only slightly taken aback then he wants to smoke, and he may get quite disturbed if he is not allowed to have a cigarette, so he feels hungry instead and buys himself some sweets or flies into a temper, or indulges himself in some other way. So if someone wants to understand himself, he must train this sixth sense, and use it to explore the unknown sides of himself, but he must do this quite fairly, without becoming personally involved. It is no use being ashamed of what one finds if it is unpleasant, just as it is no use being pleased if a good feature is discovered. We are as we are—automatic machines with good and bad features in a state of neglect through ignorance, but thanks to the sixth sense we have the possibility, if we want to, of putting ourselves into better order.

First, read this book quickly to get an impression of the ideas, then slowly several times for understanding. It is short and concentrated because it is tedious to read a long book several times. Test everything for yourself by that inner sense of truth which we all have. Only thus can truth be found. Use the same intense concentration with which a child explores its surroundings.

A child is born, a small portion of something real with a unique individuality who looks around at this strange world with a sense of wonder, and, turning its attention outwards, starts life by the acquisition of a personality. According to the responses of this individuality to the personalities of the parents and the social environment, a child learns by observation, a little that is true and a lot that is false—fairies, Father Christmas, cowboy films, love, hatred, food fads, pride, kindness, bad temper, weakness or violence—an incredible jungle. Layer upon layer is laid down as life is passed through; they form the mechanism which deals with the outside world, and takes over the sense of self. Schooling begins, the process is carried on; the child is taught what to think, what to learn, and the questions he is allowed to ask are canalized and limited.

All human beings are conditioned to assume something is real, only if it produces changes in the mind by stimulation of the senses, or extensions of the senses by various instruments. Anything else is assumed to be unreal because its existence cannot be so demonstrated. The mind is bombarded by data from the senses and by previously formed judgements about, and connections with, those sense impressions. These have always confirmed the judgements, and are often called associations. Therefore, a child brought up among people all conditioned in this way, can think and feel in no other way than through the impressions brought to his consciousness from the world outside him, or his bodily functions. It is usual for an unused organ to lose the ability to make impressions on consciousness—hence 'lazy' eyes which, though structurally normal, cannot see because their possessor has learnt to suppress the sensations from them owing to a period of enforced disuse of the eye in childhood; and deaf-mutes who, because they are born deaf, do not learn to speak unless specially taught to do so.

The awareness of being oneself—of being I—need not be derived only from the impressions gained by the senses of the outside world, or from one's body, or in the automatic associations which float up into one's consciousness as thoughts or feelings, or intuitions. Though much of the time, that occurs through the hypnotic effect of one's life and environment, it need not be so, nor is it desirable to be so, for such a state makes a human being into an automatic mass of associations ruled by his body, external events, and his previous conditioning.

Everyone has a right to be free from all this conditioning. It is a mistake to assume that one's prejudices and attitudes are fixed for ever, even though one may be very attached to them. This sort of self-satisfaction is harmful in many ways.

As the Watch Exercise is done, there is a distraction of attention by noises, movements and sensations from the body. The figures on the watch-face may attract the mind to think about the date and pass from this to consider the next thing to be done. Or the noise of a car may lead to the analysis of the make of type of the machine. Awareness of tension in the body may lead one to the realisation that one is tense and frightened. Sometimes, people want to laugh because they feel what they are being asked to do is absurd. Others will feel suspicious that they are being hypnotized. Nothing is farther from the truth. In fact, they are being induced to be more attentive and awake than usual, and will be more able to use their will than ever before. This exercise shows the performer that he can do nothing without an aim or intention. A sailing boat moves aimlessly, paying off and then coming back, head to wind, until a hand guides the rudder. Nor can anything be done if a person doesn't want to do it sufficiently to make the effort. Everything must be willed or nothing will be achieved. Even though the aim is known, inertia must be overcome. Finally, without consciousness of aim and will, body and sensations, nothing real can be achieved by the human organism. Nothing can be learnt, nor is any change of the old state possible. For example, if one wants to stop smoking, it is first necessary to have the intention of doing so. Then there must be consciousness of when it is being done, otherwise the cigarette is lit without awareness. Finally, it is necessary to want to give it up enough to go through the period of suffering before the habit dies out, and the body is rid of its addiction to tobacco smoke. Similarly, nothing can be learnt unless it is intended to take it in, and the knowledge is desired, and there is consciousness of the process of learning.

These parts of a person—aim, consciousness and will, are all close to the sense of self—what is recognized as 'I' or 'Me'. This part can watch what goes on in the mind and body. It acts as the observer who watches the thoughts, feelings, sensations, which are registered by the mind. But this state is only achieved from time to time—when really learning, when breaking a habit, or when it is artificially produced by doing the Watch Exercise.

The next move is to do this exercise until what has just been described is part of your own observation, until it is valid for you really. It's no use just reading about it. Practise it until you are familiar with the watching state and can observe thoughts and feelings floating up, as they do, into your consciousness while realizing that 'I am not my thoughts and feelings'. Do not leave off doing this until you have proven this fact to your own satisfaction. Until you have, you cannot gain insight or make observations about yourself which are valid for you. These real observations are all that matter. If you only memorized the contents of this book, you could tell someone else all about it. If he had a good memory, too, he could do the same for another. You could all then pass an examination which licenced you as qualified teachers of the Watch Exercise. But if no one had actually experienced it, there would only be memories, and thoughts about memories—theoretical stuff of no use to anyone. There is so much of this vicarious experience in life. The entertainment, education and advertising industries, books, etc., are all conveying second-hand experiences. Second-hand experience is real enough. That's what is so horrible about it. People cannot see how totally misleading it is when it is treated as reality. Most people's lives take place without aim, consciousness or will. These were present once in childhood, but have been replaced by the habits and attitudes learnt when these three essential attributes of a sense of self were plastered over by their education. In this state, people are at the mercy of the events of their lives, their circumstances, and their habits of mind. Adrift from reality, they are mental cripples. At best, zombies fitting perfectly into the social socket for which they have been deformed—at worst hopelessly insane. There are forms of disturbances that seem strange to the majority—these are labelled mad, or bad, because they are found in a minority and make difficulties for the majority. Yet the majority are just as disturbed, but in a different way. They have accepted a pattern of behaviour, to which the others they call mad, bad, or enemies, do not conform.

Until someone realizes this truth and knows from his own observation and experience that he is caught in the trap of his personality and environment, he cannot see that there is any necessity to escape from it. Another difficulty is that many people have learnt to like the cage in which they have grown up. So, changing it is a great effort for them. However, that will be the main difficulty of the so-called 'normal' people who are reading this. Those who are reading in order to help themselves because they have symptoms or emotional disturbances, will realize that the trap they are caught in is upsetting, and that it is worth trying to escape.

3

Attitudes and Ageing

NOTHING ever repeats itself exactly. The same sort of situation comes round again and again, but no events are exactly similar. Because of the general laws of creation, the similarity often seems so exact that we assume it is. But it is never so. The world spins on an oval orbit with a wobble on its axis, among a lot of planets doing the same thing in a myriad of galaxies. One of the facts of life is that everything changes all the time. There is no such thing as stability. Absolute stability is an impossibility. People who are always seeking stability, certainly find life stressful. They may become fearful, or, in trying to enforce stability where none can exist, violent.

The human mind is well equipped to cope with life. It is highly adaptable when young. As a person gets older, the ability to change or adapt becomes less, but this is not only a degeneration due to age. The apparent loss of adaptability is due to the steady accumulation of fixed attitudes, which progressively restrict the ability to respond to new situations. A child has to learn to cope with the world he lives in. He does so mostly from parents, or their substitutes, from a very early age, by storing suitable reactions and facts in his memory. Without these he could not live. A man has to earn his living, get home, and remember his relationship with his wife and children. Otherwise, he would have to be permanently looked after by an attendant or die. So memory is essential, and those who do not form an adequate one are social cripples. But among the useful memories are stored fixed attitudes such as 'Violence is permissible', 'Anger is the correct response if I am thwarted', 'Punishment is just', 'Mother is loving, Father is not', which becomes 'Women are loving, Men are not'. This is an awkward one for girls to have. 'Father (men) is kind, Mother (women) is awful', is as difficult for boys. 'Black men are dangerous', 'White men are fiends', 'Conservatives are wrong', 'Socialism is rubbish', and so on. The number of attitudes it is possible to have are innumerable. When a situation occurs, the mental 'computer' searches out the relevant attitudes from its memory bank, and brings them into consciousness with their associated feelings. This makes the individual become conscious of his reaction to the event. The trouble is that this is always based on similar older experiences. The reaction is never new, and what is presented may even be quite inappropriate for the current situation. But out it comes, and so by habit and usage, is reinforced, especially if it seems to be a successful response. In this way, the personality is built up. Stable personalities, always giving predictable responses to standard situations, are useful to Commerce and Society, and therefore highly profitable. So people are encouraged not to be individuals, and are processed by parents, schools, universities, advertising, their employers, and the State, to be useful standard citizens with known reactions. Those who do not conform tend to be poor, or even persecuted. Now there is a right time to conform, and a right time not to conform. It is absolutely necessary to develop a personality with adequate reactions to cope with society, and earn a living, so it is no use going about rebelling or drugging. This is falling into the same trap as those who feel it is necessary to impose conformity on all by force. This trap is self-righteousness. If a person feels they are right, beyond any shadow of doubt, they can use this sensation to justify the enforcement of their beliefs on others. Self-righteousness is the cause of evangelism, law, rebellion, war, and the belief that children must be brought up. A conviction that one is right makes one intolerant and isolated. Justified intolerance and isolation produce fear, because one's position of superiority and singleness is always being threatened by the others who share the world. This produces violence because the only way to maintain superiority and singleness is to live in a fortress, or drive the others away, and if they won't go, kill them.

It is necessary to realize that the feeling of self, or 'I'-ness, which leads a person to relate himself to the world, and in doing so form opinions and attitudes, is both essential and yet dangerously misleading. As long as a person has attitudes which allow him to fit in with his environment and not make excessive demands on the people around him, he will go through life without significant stress, adjusting easily to the difficulties he encounters. But suppose one of his attitudes does make him unduly demanding? Suppose that he has been spoilt by his parents who have always given into his whims and let him have everything he wanted? His life will fall below his expectations, and unless he changes, he will be put out when he does not get what he expects to be his as of right. He may become angry, frightened, or depressed, quarrel and have many jobs, or wives, before he has settled down to more appropriate responses.

As all attitudes are based on old reactions to previous similar situations, people are always indulging in unsuitable behaviour because they use some response, which was successful at one time of life, at a later period when it is not. Using the childish attitude of sitting back and letting things be done for you, which may be essential if you cannot feed or dress yourself, should change when the time comes for the bond between child and parent to dissolve. Some children go out into the world dependent, and remain lonely and sad. Some parents cannot bear to let their children go, and try either to dominate, or serve, them indefinitely, and may become depressed from grief over their apparent loss upon separation. Both should let go of each other, but remain in friendly association.

When an individual realizes that he can be fully responsible for his behaviour, thoughts and feelings, then he can observe them and not necessarily always react to them. He can, if he wants, start to give up the past. He has the possibility of abandoning the attitudes which have made difficulties for him all his life, and either making new ones, or better still reacting like a child without any attitudes at all. Then he can give every situation what it needs, free from all emotionally charged past memories.

The immediate action is to define the attitude which needs adjustment or dissolution. This requires some self-observation, or may be obtained from another person. The trouble is the other person's opinion may be biased by his attitudes. All second-hand observations must be confirmed by the individual's own judgement and observation. Accept only your own truths. Nothing else is any use to you. It is immediate observation of, and changes in the present, that is effective. Prying into the past is only useful to discover what the attitude that is being troublesome, is. The situation which produced it is often simpler, and less overlaid by others that have complicated it later, so it is easier to formulate if it is studied at the time when it first began. This is not always possible, however, for memory often fails. But the past does not matter at all. It is only the past—dead—finished with—and should be forgotten, forgiven and forsaken. It is rubbish to be got rid of.

The same applies to the unconscious mind. The distinction between the unconscious and the conscious is not important. If someone does not understand that he has fixed attitudes and is ignorant of what these attitudes are, he is ruled by them because he is unconscious of them. Hence the apparent importance of the unconscious. But once the attitude is known, its action becomes unmasked, and the reactions to it can be clearly understood. If a person has an attitude which is disturbing to the body, making this attitude conscious, imposes a barrier upon it, freeing the body. The person then copes with the reactions to the attitude at a conscious level. He suffers more emotionally, but becomes symptom-free. For example, a child has learnt that to wheeze when frightened, always produced attention and protection from his mother, as an adult he also wheezes continuously, especially when lonely. Abandoning the habit makes him at first feel more frightened and lonely than he thought he was. But if he faces this successfully, he is soon free of asthma and fear.

The psychologists who discovered the unconscious mind—Freud and Jung mainly—over-rated its iniquity and power. They were awed by its infinite diversity. Like a lot of others, they did not like what they saw. But one has to face oneself sooner or later. Though some people will break down, if forcibly confronted with their unconscious minds before they are strong enough to cope with it, this only occurs through the pressure of another person, or adverse circumstances. It never can happen if you do it yourself. The free mind is a self-protecting organisation. Learning about oneself is at times unpleasant, and hard work. But so long as you do it yourself, nothing that cannot be borne will be discovered.

A child needs love and physical care, and expects it. The characteristic attitude of a child towards life is one of expectancy and acceptance. As the child grows, the passive outlook changes to one of inquiry and self-assertion. The young person's attention turns outward, to learning about, and getting a living from, the country and people around him. This process starts at the age of three, or earlier, and goes on until about thirty-five. The attitude starts as one of self-assertion and taking, but the influence of others doing the same is considerable, so the need to exchange values, and share resources with others, must be learnt if the growing individual is to live peacefully yet independently. Positive, tolerant, relationship between people is the web of human life. Without it, existence is possible but the individual fails to thrive. If the relationship is negative or intolerant, damage is done which is more obvious in the weaker person, but just as serious in the stronger. Then there comes the period of production and adjustment. A well-adjusted person will produce more than is needed. Families are produced, savings made for old age, and new works undertaken. Middle age is a period for taking stock of oneself and making psychological adjustments. Often the individual has still got the absorption in life which is characteristic of the second phase of life, so he carries on with all his youthful activities and does not see that detachment, as well as productivity, is the desirable attitude. This period will last, for some, until their seventies, but for most until the sixties. Then comes the weakening of the body, and the personality. They are the warnings of approaching death and constitute old age, which is a preparation for dying. The need to make the final adjustments in the mind, and get free from fixed attitudes becomes more urgent. Yet many people find death frightening. It is regarded as the extinction of the personality—which it is—and, if a person believes in nothing else, the personality may become disturbed. But an individual can be sure of only one thing in life. One day he will die, so this fact had best be accepted contentedly. The fear of death is what holds hosts of people in a feverish search for ways of passing time. They fall back on youthful attitudes to do this, and the world is full of the old aping the young, holding on to money and power for dear life. Interfering with, and obstructing the young, because they cannot let go of their inappropriate attitudes. Since life is so dear, they pay a high price as well as forcing others to do the same. Their aged bodies cannot stand the emotional stress of such an existence, and they die worn out, much sooner than they might. No, old age is a return to the source of life, and should be a joyous acceptance of this fact. It is the last opportunity for making a final weeding-out of all attitudes, so that the present can be enjoyed with the loving attention that right living demands. Then it is possible to die well.

The whole of life consists of growing. Becoming old should be a continuous learning process—making the right adjustments to each stage as it comes along, and giving up old adaptations and attitudes as each stage is past. But a common attitude is that people grow up, and then stop developing. When a person 'has grown up' and 'been educated' or 'trained', that's it. Development stops. The social unit has been moulded for good. This conviction has awkward results. It fixes most people at one stage of development—the adolescent or soon after, and stops their further growth. It also makes people age earlier than they should. Not only because, as previously pointed out, youthful emotions wear out older bodies rapidly, but also because the effort of stopping natural psychological development leads to psychological contortion and eventually death; just as a plant in a confined space will do exactly the same, become deformed and die suddenly, even though supplied with adequate food, water, air and light. Quite a lot of the nervous breakdowns of middle age, and the deaths from stress diseases, are caused by failure to adapt rightly. It is not the stress of modern life that does the damage. It's the stress produced in the individual by his failure to grow and adapt according to the needs of his age and time, that kills. A constant state of learning, of awareness of the need to adapt, and respond spontaneously, free from the past—is necessary for health of mind and body.

Upsetting experiences in childhood, such as separation from parents, especially mother, by illness, accident or war, can cause a child's mind to retreat, sometimes permanently, from growing. In fact, a return to a previously well established mode of behaviour—known to be successful in dealing with life—is the normal reaction of the human being to any setback. It is called regression. A snail whips back into its shell the moment it is touched. It will be out again in a few seconds if things remain quiet. But in a human being, such a psychological retreat lasts much longer. It may take a child years to start learning again after being exposed to a hostile parent or teacher. Educational and emotional blocks, so produced, are often permanent. Children who come from disturbed or broken homes have a lot of nervous breakdowns, and behaviour problems. They have difficulties with the law, in making lasting relations with others, and in learning to adapt. But it is not these seriously deformed personalities that are important, tragic though they are. It is the delaying effect on the development of all children that the average parent and school have. This is not done only by violence. It is the self-righteousness of parents and teachers that makes them want to mould their children into little images of what they imagine they ought to be, that delays development. Think of the common phrase 'bringing up a family'. A child does not need to be 'brought up'. He should be allowed to grow up into his own potentialities. He will learn at his own rate by example. A parent should set his child an example of reasonable placid behaviour, and lovingly encourage him. Nor should a child do exactly what he wants. He must learn that there is a time for everything. All children need clear guidance given with a sort of loving indifference. A parent's child is not 'his child', but a person in his own right. The dignity of a child as an individual must be respected. The child possesses the future which a parent can never have. A child must eventually stand separate from the parent, and break the bond which attaches him to the parent when he feels able to. At this point, the parent must willingly relinquish his role and hope to remain a friend. If he has done his part well, he will. From time to time thereafter, he will be asked for advice, but should not offer it. If the separation of the child is slow, there may be an alternation of parent and friend roles for a few years, but by the early twenties, dependency of the child upon the parent should be over. If it is not, the child may not be sufficiently able, even to make a strong enough relationship with a member of the opposite sex to get married. Some never leave home. If they do get married, they depend first upon their spouse, and then upon their children, who they cannot let go emotionally when the latter grow up. Such dependent children, though adult in years and parents by the body, if not in reality, often do everything in their power to stop their children from growing up and separating from them. Luckily they do not often succeed. When the child of such a parent succeeds in breaking away from his home ties, the dependant parent often becomes unhappy, unstable, depressed, or physically ill. These remarks on parenthood have been written conventionally, as if the parent were male, but they apply even more to mothers who have the earlier, and more intimate contact with their children than fathers. However, the role of a father is of equal importance in the function of a balanced personality, especially from the age of three onwards. Each parent contributes the male and female characteristics from which the child can make a selection according to sex and unique individuality.

4

The Human Animal

UNLESS a person's attention is increased and widened so that he can be aware of more than his sense impressions, he cannot do more than just notice these states. He cannot understand how they came about. He only experiences the reactions and behaves according to his training. There is no possibility of changing the response. He is his instinctive reactions. He responds reflexly to the usual animal drives as modified by his past experiences, and is aware of no other possible response. He lives in a state of light hypnosis, in which sleeping and waking alternate. Providing he remains comfortable, and is not aware of having a problem, or is not challenged, he ticks over automatically, according to his training and instincts, just like an animal. Unlike the animal, he has a much more highly developed brain which acts like a computer, and can process complex thoughts and feelings. But most of the time, these are not used at all. It is only when he has a problem, or is uncomfortable, that he may use his powers to alter his reactions. Usually he does not, and becomes disturbed emotionally. If he does, his behaviour can alter a lot—but only in terms of the events that caused the check, and his habits of mind. Nothing new comes in, but a choice between alternatives can be made—to wear this or that, to marry or not, and so on. A well trained mind can work out complex problems—how to go to the moon, for instance. Nothing new in terms of basic knowledge has been used. It is just the response of a group of human animals to the fear of invasion of their territory, and the exploratory drive. Since most people's lives are spent in reacting automatically to their drives, fixed attitudes, and external events just as an animal does, it would seem to be useful to examine these drives, as well as the pastimes and games with which the naked ape fills his time. The reason for this is that if some of the drives are excessively developed, or the games which started as simple pastimes get too complex, or are played too seriously or for too high stakes, there is trouble.

Some people's view of human psychology is based only on seeing man as an animal, but man is not just his behaviour. He is not only an ape. Yet, it is worth while seeing what a clever ape he can be, and how complex. Because it is good for human pride to realize that most of his greatest material achievements are still only apish tricks which distract attention from his real purpose.

The motives that govern animal behaviour have been studied particularly in the last few decades by zoologists. They can be thought of as appetites or drives—basic needs which govern all animal activity. They are hunger, territory or possession, inertia, exploration, sex and contact. Each animal has a memory store and also some capacity for imagination. Simple games of make-believe such as mock fights, and tag, are often played by many different species.

Hunger

The need for food and drink is as compelling as the need for air. We would die if deprived of either; in a few minutes without air, after some days in the case of water, after some weeks in the case of food alone. Food must be hunted or found, grown or reared. We need just enough to keep us in health and provide replacement energy for work done. Relatively more is needed in childhood when growth is greatest, and less in old age when body requirements and energy output are least. The correct attitude to food is that we should eat to live, and enjoy doing that, but no more.

Disturbances of eating are common. Most people in the western world overeat. They get emotional satisfaction from food, and use this as a substitute for the former, when they are upset. The satisfaction gained at the breast by a baby is not just in milk alone, and is often substituted for by mothers who plug their babies with a bottle, or a dummy to keep them quiet, and later give them a sweet on the first sign of complaint. They don't bother to find out what the child wants—love, protection, handling, safety, mothering in fact. A low standard of noise tolerance, or a lack of interest on the part of the parent—deprives the child of the security, and love needed to establish his confidence in his own abilities, and establishes a low standard of resistance to the problems of separate existence. The parental policy outlined above trains a child to satisfy an emotional upset of any sort with the oral satisfaction of eating. It's no wonder that adults reared in this style of short or no breast feeding, overeat, as well as feel deprived.

Food fads—the dislike of this or that article of diet are even more common. 'Little Johnny can't eat bacon, it's so fat and greasy to him—but he loves butter.' 'My Peter can only eat frozen peas, all other vegetables upset his tummy'—(clearly an obstinate and cautious fellow). 'I'm sure I'm allergic to milk. It's so white and horrible. I feel sick when I look at it.' (But she likes pink ice-cream.) So it goes on—you name it, someone can't eat it. Of course a few people have genuine food sensitivities, but they don't eat what upsets them because it does make them gripe, get diarrhoea, or come out in a rash. They often like the foods they know by experience must be avoided. The faddist who dislikes a food is upset by the sight of it and never eats it. Nearly all the people who can't eat a certain food do so for emotional reasons. Some have their fads imposed on them by their parents, others develop them as a defence against parents. The food fad being an effective way of non-cooperation, allowing the individual to impose his will. The threat of clearing up the vomit, coupled with the fear of letting their darling starve and failing in their duty, soon gets the young rebel his way. This sort of struggle often goes on in adult life between partners in marriage, between doctors and patients, who relate themselves with each other through eating, bargaining over this or that item as if life depended on it. It is important sometimes of course, but mostly it's a form of communication.

Apart from the always underrated dangers of obesity in the weak-willed, there is also danger in having too strong a control over the appetite. There are people who starve themselves to death or into serious illness, either deliberately in a hunger strike, or unconsciously, because they are emotionally disturbed but suppress this, and only experience a compulsive dislike of food. There are people whose appetites, while not so desperately affected by their unconscious mind, are superficially sensitive. A harsh word, a sudden worry, or idea, will stop some people dead in the middle of a meal, or even a mouthful. A few moments later they may be happy again, often after suitable coaxing, best done without display, and they are off on the next course, or make up for it by eating sweets later. Sometimes people develop a deficiency disease unintentionally because of a fad, out of ignorance, or poverty. For instance, they may have an idea that animal food is bad and develop a protein deficiency, or that only milk and potatoes suit their ulcer, and develop vitamin deficiencies, or dislike all fruit and vegetables and do the same.

Territory

Most animals have a territory, within which they are dominant and feel safe. There is an urge to maintain the area in which he finds his food, as his own, by marking it out so that others keep out, and to defend it. As an animal gets farther away from the centre of his territory, the drive weakens. Some animals, chiefly the dangerous ones who live off other animals do not have a fixed territory, but live among their prey, and this situation is very much the same with human beings. Everyone feels safer at home and takes a pride in it. Some people are so frightened, they cannot leave it. Many children and some adults become ill if they move house. Some old people become so attached to the few pieces of furniture that constitute home, that they cannot bear to leave the place, and stay there, living miserably, long after they have ceased to be able to look after themselves adequately. Once relinquishment of their 'territory' becomes inevitable, they become depressed and many die, or have an illness shortly after a removal.

For many men, money is the substitute for territory. Money buys property, but can become an aim in itself. To hold territory, power is needed. Larger and more powerful animals have the larger areas of land. For many men, power is a substitute for territory. To some, money buys power, but to others safety. They are not interested in power. Those who like power will manœuvre endlessly and skilfully to get their own way, to dominate, to force their will on others, but have not got the slightest interest in money or land—their 'territory' is other people. Women do this just as much as men, but they are more subtle about it; their field is mostly in the home, and their subjects children, or men. A good example of this is found in the play *Candida* by George Bernard Shaw. Like all drives, enough of the urge to possess is needed to make a living. But to spend a life amassing territory in order to feel safe, or in order to dominate, or to live to dominate, or to be unable to live except in one place surrounded by certain things, is clearly either to have too much of it, or to be utterly dependent upon the territorial drive.

Exploration

All animals have an urge to find out as much as they can of their surroundings. They examine anything new in it, to see what its properties are—dangerous, eatable, safe, and so on. Like all the drives, too much exploration or exploration as an end in itself, can be dangerous. It can lead to having too large an area to protect. Lots of explorers have died by going too far into inhospitable lands and seas, unprepared. The intention to expand, to explore, at any price, leads to poverty at home and insufficient attention to the problems there. As an example of this, the two leaders—and only real rivals in the space race—Russia and America—also have extreme poverty and severe human problems at home. On the other hand, lack of the drive to explore will lead to the failure to exploit opportunities and develop natural talents. It is no use being intelligent if this is not used to explore possibilities. It is realized nowadays, though not by all, that the possession of a high degree of intelligence is not as important as being able to use what one has to inquire. In fact, a person who persistently inquires and explores may learn more and get more out of life than a person who is more intelligent but who has less urge to explore. The latter is likely to do better than the former in a school, where there is organized pressure to learn, but when education is over, the former deals with life better.

Inertia
The Won't Factor

In a way, it can seem that inertia is the opposite of exploration. If the drive to explore is nil, one can be inert. But if the quality of exploration is contrasted with quality of inertia, the difference becomes clear. Inertia is resistance to change. Exploration does not necessarily involve change, while inertia can be a state that exists when all the other drives are absent and everything is quiet in the surroundings (that is, a passive state), but inertia is also an active resistance. It could be called the Won't Factor.

Like all the other drives, having the right amount of inertia—neither too much, nor too little, is important. Have too much and you are obstinate, a rabid conservative reactionary, whose rigid inability to change or learn new reactions, quite rightly maddens those who have to deal with you. In fact, if carried too far in early childhood, inertia may lead to a defective formation of the personality. It could be that mental deficiency and even autism are produced by a resistance to learning, produced by excessive inertia. On the other hand, too little resistance to change will produce an excessively responsive person who cannot hold on to one idea long enough to achieve anything. Society would be unstable and chaotic if composed of such people.

Sex

Sex is a strong force. It can be as irresistible to animals as the attraction which brings together positive and negative electrical charges is to electrons. Its result in the state of nature is the creation of a new member of the species, which should come about as a result of a joyous union of the parents. But like all the instinctive drives, it tends to become distorted. It may be undervalued or overvalued. The pleasurable aspect can be divorced from the creative, and the former pursued as an end in itself. As a part of overvaluation, the intellect can manipulate the natural processes of the sex act and can think up all sorts of variations. A certain amount of this is normal, but some products of the intellect and imagination are so strange, and their connection with fear, and violence (the desire to suffer or cause others to suffer), so great, that the element of love and mutual affirmation of the partners as human beings is completely lacking, and they have to be labelled perversions. They can only be the product of a distorted personality.

However, more people undervalue sex and suffer from fear of it, or find it repugnant because they feel violated by it, than those who overvalue it. Most people who fear sex do not complain much or feel a sense of loss. People tend to assume their own experience is normal. Rejection of sexuality leads to the attitude that sex is an unpleasant subject, not 'nice' to discuss. The children of parents with this attitude are exposed to a tacit rejection of sex, and the responses of their parents to questions on the subject are limited, frightened or frightening. Children who are parent acceptors adopt the same attitude. The parent rejectors may become too experimental and overvalue sex. Too early experimentation with sex in an atmosphere of parental sex rejection may stimulate the individual into excess activities. As this usually occurs at an age when parenthood is financially and socially undesirable, and in the first strong flood of sexuality, the pleasurable side of sex becomes overvalued, and the creative aspects repressed. So that what is really a vital act of affirmative union, expressive of a creative relationship between two people can become of no more value than a nocturnal emission.

In order to allow people to develop a healthy sexuality, a change in the present social attitudes towards sex would help. Co-education should be the rule. The natural desire of children to investigate sex organs should not be condemned. Time, and facilities, for this mutual education, as well as for their juvenile affairs, should be a normal part of school activity. Advice must be only on demand, and totally informal. It should be channelled to specially selected sexually mature teachers. Sexuality cannot be learnt from 'Sex Education' lessons. It should be openly acknowledged, and allowed to develop in the individual's own time. But good sex and contraceptive techniques need to be taught by a skilful and experienced person, so there should be classes in those aspects of sex, where for example, the importance of clitoris stimulation in facilitating orgasm in women can be learnt. Contraception should be readily available free of charge to all, from puberty to the age of legal adulthood. These new attitudes should be put into practice in special pre-school play groups, for normal children become sexually aware between nine and eighteen months. There is no period when sexuality is latent, if sexuality is not repressed. The so-called 'Latent Period' is the product of a sexually repressive society. The above measures would allow a partial escape for children from the restrictive attitudes of repressive parents. Because there are a majority of such people, these changes are not likely to be adopted. It would need a dictator to effect them in a short time. So, in a situation where, for many people a close relationship with the opposite sex is actively discouraged by parents, schools and the law, it is inevitable that the young should manipulate their own sex organs in order to obtain relief from sexual tension. And a certain amount of masturbation by both sexes is universal, and harmless. When the right partner appears, and regular sexual intercourse becomes possible, it dies away. In order to counteract the oppressive attitudes of the past towards masturbation, it is fashionable to speak of it as if it were normal. But this is an overcompensation. It is normal behaviour, and certainly nothing to be ashamed of, or guilty about, as it may be the only practical outlet for the sex drive. But it is not normal sex, and it does have its dangers.

Masturbation is an act of self-stimulation and satisfaction of oneself, by oneself. It does not involve consideration and union with another person. It is a sterile act, not an exchange between two bodies and minds in an act of love to achieve a new life. Fixation in this selfish emotional position can prevent the making of a satisfying sex relationship with another person. This can occur if an individual does not fall in love soon after puberty, and masturbation becomes the sole outlet for the sex drive. Intercourse between two people who remain fixed in the masturbatory attitude to sex is no more than mutual masturbation. The resultant orgasm is felt only in the penis in the male, and the clitoris in the female. There is no emotional giving to each other—no real relationship occurs. Couples can live apparently full sex lives in this state. Sex is a personal experience, and it is not often that people discuss and look into their sex responses. They accept what they experience as normal and may not realize what they are missing. The emotionally sterile mutual masturbatory sex act is more common than is realized. It is the sort of person one is that determines the quality of the orgasm. It is not the other way about as Freud had it.

The quality and intensity of the orgasm varies considerably among individuals and couples. The mildest experience is a pleasurable pulsation involving the penis or clitoris only. In more intense forms the sensation spreads, first to the pelvis, and may be to involve the whole body. There is a feeling of expansion of oneself and union with the partner, and to a variable degree a loss of the normal consciousness. There are visions like whirling kaleidoscope lights. This stage may be accompanied by wild behaviour in excitable people. Finally, though this is rare, there may be, in addition to the other sensations, a sense of leaving the body and of an ecstatic vibratory union with one's partner felt in the region of the heart, yet outside the body. Once experienced this is never forgotten. It may occur only once in a relationship. Many circumstances must be right for its achievement, but no couple who has had this experience of orgasm fail to regard it as the acme of their union. It follows from the above that orgasms vary a great deal in time, quality, and intensity, even with one couple. But people who have never experienced more than the first degree may be missing something they could achieve, and should consider whether they need to improve their attitude to sex, technique of intercourse, or emotional relationship, or all three.

Everyone has fears of failing to fulfil his or her sexual role. In fearful people this can be a severe handicap. Ignorance of what is involved in sex, parental rejection of sex, unfortunate childhood experiences involving sex, and the trap of masturbation, all combine to produce a low degree of sexual response. Absolute impotence is rare. In men this may grade through evasive behaviour, inability to raise an erection, premature ejaculation, inability to achieve ejaculation of the seed, on to ejaculation without the satisfaction obtained by masturbation. In women impotence may start with behaviour which makes penetration of the vagina impossible, from a downright refusal, spasm of the thighs, or vaginal muscles, or all three. But after penetration is permitted, lack of sensation is the usual form of female impotence, and is common. Such a woman does not achieve an orgasm. It should be clear that a life of frequent intercourse, and childbearing may be lead by an impotent woman who loves her husband, and does it to oblige, or only to have a family. This state is perpetuated often by ignorance of the importance of gentle stimulation of the clitoris as a preliminary to sexual intercourse in the vagina, or by selfishness on the part of the man, who is only interested in thrusting away to his orgasm, without consideration of his partner's needs.

Some people become intolerant of sexual intercourse through becoming disgusted with sex because of their own impotence, and deny their partners a satisfactory sex life. Sometimes they do this by becoming violent, and ultimately drive their partners away. This is more common in men. Sometimes they freeze out the sex urge of the other member of the couple, until they also become impotent. The latter ploy allows the relationship to go on, though there is often a compensatory development of a physical or mental disorder. For example, one woman suffered a nervous breakdown because she could not cope with the slight, and timid sexual 'demands' of her husband. Her illness so frightened him that he decided to contain himself, for each time he approached her, her self-control would go and signs of the 'mental illness' would return. However, she still wanted him to share a 4-foot bed and pet her, which he found upsetting. Finally, he got out of this by developing asthma which kept her awake at night, so he was able to insist on separate rooms 'for her sake'. Unfortunately, this situation prevented him ever losing his asthma completely, though it improved as he understood the situation better. However infidelity is the usual solution to this situation, but in an inhibited society its practical solution represents difficulties.

The act of sex is so surrounded with fear, guilt and violence, that mutual adjustment between a couple is more difficult than is realized. People are seldom frank about sex. In order to achieve a satisfactory sex life, there should be frankness and kindness, consideration and permissiveness towards variations of sexual behaviour between partners, in order that both should achieve as much satisfaction as is possible. But striving after perfection should not be carried to extremes. It can lead to the break-up of marriages which are right in every other way, and lead to failure to achieve satisfaction ultimately. It can even prevent anyone making more than a transient relationship, in the endless search for the satisfaction he, or she, will never get. Perfection can be a legitimate aim, but to strive for it in sex, never. To let go—to merge in the other, to abandon oneself to, and in, the act of sex, brings the joy.

Sex is only one of several instinctive drives. It is not the central driving force of the personality, as some make the mistake of believing. But it is something special. That is why people think about it so much, or try to deny it so hard.

Although some time has been spent describing what isn't real sex and some of the difficulties and variants. They are of no importance. They attract those who are mentally abnormal. In fact, if you have specially turned to this section on sex, this is proof that you have a sex problem. Try and discover what it is. There is an old saying—'Those who talk do not know, those who know do not talk.' In most books on sex the real meaning and benefit of sexual crisis, or orgasm, is not mentioned. The sensual side is over-emphasized, in fact if you believed them you might get the idea that sex was no more than pleasantly lubricated friction between the sex organs of two gymnasts, and people take drugs, mainly cannabis (pot or marijuana, hashish) to enhance this aspect. Of course, that side is very pleasant—but that's not the point. In real sexual union, with two people of the opposite sex giving themselves utterly to each other, they are freed from their personalities for a moment of time. They shed the rigid control of their sense of 'I', their attitudes, their problems. In such a sexual union, a couple is nearer to God or whatever equivalent is used, nearer to what is not 'I' in themselves, than at any other time. That is why people value sex so much. But it is not often that the average couple achieve this state of bliss in mutual orgasm to its full extent. Much has to be right before this can happen. Time, circumstances, attitude to sex, to each other, and a great deal of attention, must be present in the act. However, there is enough of the numinous, shocking, epileptic quality about lesser degrees of orgasm to make people either very attracted, or very repelled by sex, when their personalities are so strong that they find a temporary loss of normal consciousness too frightening to face. To people who have this experience, the similarity between the results of sexual orgasm and a 'good trip' with the group of hallucinating drugs derived from certain fungi ('Acid', LSD, mescaline, etc.) are obvious. The experience is certainly not of the ordinary physical world. Other modes of perception are experienced. Though the result of a sex orgasm may be physically tiring, it is vitalizing psychologically. Those for whom sex goes really well are usually healthy, and do not get tangled up by mental problems for long.

The group of hallucinating drugs just mentioned can be used to expand widely, and enhance, all forms of experience, including sex. The idea of taking a drug to produce an experience that one may not be able to achieve in ordinary life, may be frightening. But, if guided by someone experienced in suitable surroundings, one may become accustomed to new states of mind, and find that the response to sex is greatly improved. On the other hand, being forced, by taking a substance not naturally available to the body, to have an experience that cannot be withstood, may destroy an individual, especially someone who is unstable, and who is alone in unsuitable surroundings. A few people are ready to have the 'doors of perception' opened artificially—for the majority this is too stressful, or they would rather not. But it can happen naturally, safely, and joyfully in real sex, without any artificial aids. This is a state so ecstatic that it is worth great effort to achieve. Sex can be holy communion.

Knowledge—Memory

Memory is a store of experience. It is by relating some new event to previous experience, that knowing comes about. Thinking is a form of comparing one item of knowledge with another. Memory is the store of items of thinking about experience. Nothing new comes out of it. Though apparently new combinations can be produced, the basic units—the bricks of which they are made, are always old.

All creatures have a memory. In some of them it is possible to teach them a trick and then graft with a bit of its body, the ability to perform this trick from one animal to another. The human brain is a computer as well as a memory bank, which is so much more complex than other simple animals, that it is difficult to imagine that the same could occur in humans. But the fact that people from all over the world, from widely different cultures, have similar dream images, shows that an inherited memory is present in all of us. So does the early flowering of musical and graphic artistic ability, which runs in certain families.

Imagination and Fantasy

Since the basic ideas in a person's mind are either inherited or learnt, nothing really new enters into mental activity. But it can be argued that some products of the imagination are new, because they have not been thought of before. This is true, but only in so far as they are new combinations of old things. It is like the kaleidoscope, the number of patterns multiplied by reflection seem infinite for practical use, but are not. Imagination can be used to solve problems without spending time and money, but should always be tested by experience. When imagination turns away from the practical, from what is possible to what is impossible, it becomes fantasy.

The test of what is real nowadays, is that if it is not communicable it is unreal. Many people use that as a test of reality. They say, if I cannot verify your experience by repeating your assertion myself, what you say is not true. In other words, if the experience cannot be transmitted from person to person, it is not true. This works well in the physical world, and is the basis of the scientific method. But in the mental world, this sort of proof of reality is not possible. One person can have experiences which are not possible to another. This is because we are all unique beings. For example, consider psychic phenomena. Some people get visions of those close to them when they are going to, or have just, died. This is common. But you cannot communicate the ability to verify this to another person. It can only be experienced. So a disbeliever will never be able to accept or prove to his satisfaction that such things happen unless he has such an experience himself. Communication is a fashionable word now. If you tell something to an unbelieving person which is your own experience, he will call his failure to believe you, a failure on your part to communicate. You can see this happening at most open religious discussions. To sum up, some reality is not verifiable by communicable experiment. It can only be verified by experience which is not transmissible from person to person. Reality is not confined to that which is verifiable by experiment.

However, imagining the impossible is a common human failing. People misuse the facility of imagination to fulfil their wishes in fantasy. A common form of fantasy is imagining someone else is responsible for your own failure or unpleasant feelings, and blaming it on him. Another example is finding an excuse that is not true for doing something you do not want to do, and then acting it out, or finding a reason for justifying something you want to do, and acting as if it was so. For example, people often imagine a physical sex relationship with another person. Mostly this is a normal one, but often is unusual. In fact the sexual fantasies that some people have can be so odd that they pass the bounds of the most fantastic creations imaginable. The trouble is that continuously indulged fantasy may become a fixed habit necessary to the person to complete the sex act. And not only necessary for sex—but for living, and this is one of the ways into madness. Everyone has fantasies to a certain degree. A person who states he has none is either lying, or suppresses and forgets very easily. But for those who indulge in fantasy and live in their imagination—illness, fatigue, the taking of chemicals, especially those classed as drugs, stress of any sort—mental or physical, may result in fantasy dominating the consciousness of that person. The fantasies then become more real than the sense impressions of the outside world, or the emotional fantasy more real than the usual feelings and reactions of that person, who then believes and behaves as if his fantasies were real. This is a state of hallucination. If they are very odd hallucinations, the subject is considered mad. But some hallucinations are much more socially acceptable. They are the ones described above as fantasies needed as substitutes for living a normal life. For instance, a young man has a fantasy that he is much more capable than he really is. He imagines he can be a great business man—run affairs—direct large enterprises—be powerful, have plenty of money, and mistresses and so on. He directs all his energies into these fields, and neglects his job, wife and family. He is always trying to bring off the above aims, and applies for many jobs, which may lead to fulfilling his desires. He doesn't do well in the jobs he gets, because he has not the capacity for them. He fails to get promoted, and finds the duties stressful. He is always under pressure, anxious, and angry. Anything can go wrong with such a person. He may get attacks of fainting, or an ulcer if he is passive, and conscientious, or he will desert his wife, and children if he is a bolter, or have a depression if he gives up.

Contact

One of the needs of the human animal essential for its existence is contact with others, preferably of the same kind, though not necessarily. Prisoners in solitary confinement may stave off the mental breakdown which this may precipitate, by taking a pet. Children fail to thrive, and die if deprived of handling, or an emotional exchange with their attendants. In one ill-fated, though well-intentioned institution, all the children treated in this way had died of one condition or another in three years. Exactly the same occurs in animals, treated in the same way. The need for the exchange of contact through body and mind between humans, is as essential a drive as hunger. Without it, we shrivel, but deprivation of contact is only fatal in months or years for babies. In the young, it deforms the personality, and the prisons, mental hospitals, divorce courts, and skid rows are full of the unfortunates who suffered emotional deprivation when young. There is no one who can endure isolation without being severely stressed.

It is no surprise, therefore, to find that fantasy can be used as a substitute for emotional intercourse. Most people in solitary confinement find they can hold on to reality and not suffer hallucinations, by imagining familiar people or places, and carrying on a mental exchange with them. Lonely people, not in confinement, obtain satisfying emotional exchange by inventing a ritual or game involving more than one player. Some of these are imitations of a real human activity, like war or hunting, but others are artificial like golf, but underlying all games there is contest. So it could be said that they are all a form of war. Recently, it has been pointed out that many forms of social intercourse take the form of games. Some are played at parties only, but many are life games, played for high stakes, even life itself. Some people cast themselves for life in the role of a games player, and their behaviour is only comprehensible if the game is known. They develop artificial parts of their personalities, based on a fantasy, which may dominate, even ruin their lives. Look no further than the alcoholics, gamblers, and self-righteous who have voluntarily given their lives for the glory of a cause, blinded by their self-cast role as hero or martyr.

Roles

Four of the roles that people may make themselves play have just been mentioned—alcoholic, gambler, hero and martyr. This tendency to play roles goes far beyond those needed for games. A baby inevitably has to play the role of a child. He learns from his parents, and so also inevitably becomes like them, so his next main role is 'parent'. This may not become apparent until he also becomes a parent, when the tendency is to behave like, or directly unlike, one's parents towards one's children. But the young person learns from many other people he meets; copying this or that attitude in the same way. Teachers, actors, friends, characters in plays, books, history, all form the models from which a person builds up the repertoire of the roles he will play in his life.

If you do not believe that this is so, ask yourself whether you behave in the same way to your mother or your father, your parents or your teachers, your teachers or your friends, your friends or your wife or husband, your wife and your boss, your boss and your mates or those you boss. Are you exactly the same person to all of them? Of course not. You play a different role, and often a different game, with most of them.

Useful observations to make are to spot your roles and games, using the ability to observe cultivated by the watch exercise. A good account of many well verified human games has been given by Dr. Eric Berne in his book *Games People Play*. There are more in *Put Offs and Come-ons*, a book by Dr. A. Chapman.

The way a child learns is by imitation. But he cannot imitate until he can observe, make an aim to learn, and want to do so enough to persist until he succeeds. You can see this in action as soon as he finds out the benefit he gets from saying 'Ma-Ma', and in learning to walk. Children are in the state of observing, which can be relearnt by doing the watch exercise, from soon after birth. They lose the faculty as they learn their roles, and begin to play their games 'for real'. Then their attitudes harden. They cease to see the events of their lives, and relations with other people, except through these, often fantastic, constructions of other imaginary people. These ways of taking in reality become fixed and the individual ceases to be able to perceive things and others as they really are. Of course, for most people the ability to learn is not wholly lost, it's dulled and misused. By effort and following the instructions in the first chapters, it can be relearnt, and used to change the personality. Not entirely—that would not be worth the effort, but enough to change the one or two really troublesome attitudes, and to give up the dangerous roles.

There is another way to acquire behaviour patterns. The complicated behaviour of animals is not learnt in the way described above. Every animal has an inborn pattern of behaviour characteristic of its species, and sex. But this only develops if the right triggers are met at the right times to set these patterns of behaviour going. If the appropriate sequence does not happen, there may be an absence of the behaviour necessary to survive, or an unusual sort of behaviour for that animal develops. A lamb which has lost its mother and been artificially fed always recognizes its foster-mother, and will come out of the flock and greet that person whenever he comes into the field, so long as it is still young. Normal lambs never behave in this way. Ducks can be made homosexual, and induced to become attached to humans, or wooden model ducks, by exposing them to the appropriate stimulus at the right time of their lives. Female monkeys reared in isolation, neglect their children, and may even kill them. But pregnancy has a socializing effect, and subsequent offspring are better treated.

The same mechanism of imprinting operates in humans as in animals. The ways in which it does have not been explored yet, but will yield some fundamental information about the personality. There cannot be much doubt that the basic attitudes towards male and female, and the urge to form a personality, and to learning of the mimicking type are a part of the instinctive imprinting of the human animal. That is why, when they go wrong, as in homosexuality, and autism, the abnormality is so resistant to all forms of treatment.

The different roles that make up a single personality can be grouped under three main headings. First, the child, then the parent, and finally the adult. The first is creative, playful, and is the product of the basic characteristic of the child reacting with the parents and other components of the childish world. It is the part of us that likes games. The parent is the part that has been acquired by learning and imprinting from the real parents, and other people who have acted as parents in the life of the person. The roles tend to be directing, repressive, and dominating. They are the parts of the personality which lead or drive. The object upon whom the parent acts may be the individual himself, when the action is introverted or turned inwards, or other persons when the action is turned outwards or extroverted. Both the parent and the child get excited by their activity. If things go well for them, they are joyous. If things go wrong they are upset, angry, frustrated or violent, according to what is appropriate. They bring happiness and trouble into the life of the individual. They are essential older parts of the personality, but it is better to be able to take a detached view of them, and not be dominated by their incessant reactions. The part of oneself which forms later is the adult, and this has the ability to look with the necessary detachment from the emotional reactions of the child and parent. The adult gives the situation what it needs. He does not react personally to the situation and always try and impose his own views on it as the child or parent would.

Displacement Activities

If an animal cannot express any of the drives described above, an alternative outlet for their pent-up energy which would have been used up in that drive, occurs. There may be aimless repetitive movements, fidgeting, tearing things up, or tearing oneself up, like nail-biting and scratching. Masturbation, when upset, is a good example of displacement of the need for, say, social intercourse, or say, a frustrated desire to explore. Several more examples have already been given in the descriptions of the various drives. Animals have a limited range of displacement activities and these are best observed in captivity and when they are overcrowded. Man has an almost infinite capacity for finding alternative mental and external activities. His adaptability is amazing. In fact, it could be said that his excessive tendency to be adaptable while being the secret of his fantastic exploitation of the Earth's produce, is also the cause of his failure to develop it successfully. This very adaptability also produces a strong tendency for him never to react to things as they are. It is so much more easy for him to adapt by producing an evasive reaction, that his personality becomes a means of evading reality.

5
Thinking and Feeling
The Emotions Classified

THERE are several sorts of mental activity lumped together under the word 'thinking'. If someone becomes aware of a difficulty, and you ask him what he is doing about it, he will reply that he is thinking it out. He may be frightened of it, or angry about it, or be so happy he is not affected by it; he may be comparing it with his past experience, and working out a solution; he may be observing his body's reactions to the problem—that is his instinctive response, or be adapting himself to the new situations by changing his reactions. It is not important to go into this in detail. As long as thinking and feeling are distinguished, that is enough. All the other forms of mental activity are variations of these two, affected by time, change, inertia, and whether applied to body processes, the animal drives, or the human activities of man.

Thinking was mentioned before as a process of comparison, by which some new situation is assessed in terms of what is already in the mind—in memory. In this way, any really new event is presented to consciousness, not as a truly new occurrence, but only in terms of the already known. It may seem new, and be recorded as new in the memory—but thought acts like a filter cutting out all but the already known. Thinking has a stabilizing effect, but it also encases the mind in a rigid cage that is totally limiting.

Emotion has a different quality from thought, one of valuing or desire. It acts much faster than thought. When you meet someone, you at once feel whether you like him or not. Later you may more slowly work out why, by comparing his characteristics with other people you know, using thought. So feeling influences thought, and may be tolerant or intolerant—in this example, liking or disliking. If you have positive feelings about someone or something, you think positively too, choosing favourable comparisons. If you dislike someone, that is feel negatively towards him, you also think negatively, producing disadvantageous comparisons from your memory stores.

So far, emotion has been described as a feeling involving valuation, and attraction or repulsion, a state of mind involving opposite possibilities. Emotion is not the same as what is called getting emotional about something. That is a common phrase which usually means becoming disturbed emotionally in an intolerant way, and calling the physical reaction to the preceding emotional state 'getting emotional'. The physical reactions to fear—trembling, shaking, sweating, feeling cold or hot, wanting to pass water or open the bowels, are not fear. The reactions to anger—flushing, seeing red, the heart pounding, the instinctive desire to fight, are not anger itself. The feeling has preceded the reactions of the body—which are instinctive, not emotional. Emotion as well as being fast, has a much lighter elusive quality than these. You notice the lightness much more with positive emotions, such as hope and charity, though these also often have a physical reaction. People are so much more aware of their bodies than their feelings, that they treat their bodies' reactions as reality—as themselves. They just are their physical reactions. So they are unable to perceive their emotions. They are accustomed to modifying their bodies' reactions with all sorts of comforts—warming, cooling, massaging, painting it, feeding, giving it sweets or salty things, soothing it with tobacco, alcohol or coffee, to mention only a few of the social drugs, let alone the host of mood changers and sleeping pills pushed legally by the doctors, and the illegal drugs. It is not surprising, therefore, that they get hooked by the drugs which have the property of making people crave them once they have had a few doses; then eventually start taking the harder addictive drugs in combination, to get a stronger effect. This is a horrible state to get into—a living death, which mercifully often ends in physical death. But too much attention is paid to the end stages—when it is too late.

Addiction would not occur if people took responsibility for their emotional states. This is easier said than done, but the first step is to learn to apprehend one's own emotions, and then to learn the range of emotions possible to man. After this, it requires some hard work to develop deficient emotions, and transform negative ones. Before going further, it is necessary to realize that words used to convey meaning are inadequate messengers—especially when dealing with emotions. The words used for the emotions to be described, are just symbols. They are not the emotions themselves. Try to make out the meaning behind the words in yourself, or in your direct experience of others.

There are three positive emotions—faith, hope and charity. These are old terms taken from St. Paul's First Epistle to the Corinthians. Though no religious content is especially intended, this does not exclude these emotions being used in this sense if desired. These terms have been used because they are the best words in English for the emotions they designate, and are in common usage.

Faith is awareness of the universal pattern. It gives a sense of belonging to a state of order. Through faith one has the inner certainty, that no matter how baffling a situation may seem, it has meaning. Faith gives pliant firmness to the person who has it. Not a rigid static stability, but a flexible response to constantly changing situations. It confers a sense of belonging, and leads to an aspiration to be a part of the whole—to share in the overall design, and not impose one's own ideas of what the design may be, on the existing situation. It gives humbleness, and has to do with possessing a sense of direction. It is the feeling corresponding to aim. Faith is the inner certainty of there being a higher power.

Hope is the energy of optimism. It is an expectancy of good. Whereas faith has to do with intention, hope has more to do with awareness. It is the feeling equivalent to consciousness. It provides a constant source of energy to the mind. Whereas faith penetrates, hope provides the energy to drive on over a broad front. It is expansive in character.

Charity is a unifying force. It is the word used to translate the Greek word *charis* in the authorized version of the New Testament. It is not used here in the modern sense of giving alms to the needy, though this is what a person in a state of charity would do. Perhaps the Mediterranean *caritas*, or *charisma* are better equivalents, but are not as English as charity. There is therefore in it, an attracting together, and mutual joining in unity. So giving, taking, and acceptance are found in charity. It is the emotion which is commonly called love. But that word is not used to signify charity here for two reasons. At one extreme the meaning of love has been debased to describe the instinctive responses of sexual attraction, which it is not; at the other, it is necessary to have a word equivalent to what is called *agape* in the Greek New Testament. It would be cumbersome to use the word love instead of charity here, and then qualify it later by saying that there is also higher love, transcendental love, or spiritual love. To qualify the sublime is impossible. Therefore charity will be used here, and love in the last chapter. Charity has two aspects, giving and acceptance. To experience it fully both aspects must be realized. It is not possible to give wholly, without being able to accept completely. Charity is needed for care and understanding. It is not possible to keep up a relationship without charity. It is a maintaining, bringing together force. Though faith will supply aim, and hope consciousness, it is not possible to sustain mental activity without the force of will given by charity. So this emotion sustains the will.

At equal strength, these three positive feelings give a balance to the activity of the mind that ensures appropriate reactions to any event. If one always gave each situation what it needed, there would never be any difficulty in personal relationships. But, of course, it is not like that often. People start off in a state of unbalance, lacking in the ability to experience, one, two or all these emotions. Or they may start life equipped with them, and lose them through their experience. If they don't lose them, they learn disturbances of the normal positive emotions, which seem appropriate because they are not aware of any other possibility. One way this happens is through the switch to the opposite reaction which occurs when people are stressed beyond the limits they can stand. It was first recorded by Pavlov. He had trained dogs to salivate when they heard a bell ring, because this sound was always followed by their food. This was his famous conditioned reflex. One day after the bell had been sounded, a water pipe broke, and the kennels were flooded. The expectant salivating dogs were nearly drowned. After this some of them reacted by howling, or barking and showing fear, whenever the bell rang. There had been a reversal of their reaction to the trigger of the conditioned reflex. Later it was shown that the opposite could also happen. A pleasureable response could be induced to an unpleasant stimulus. This information is made use of in brainwashing. The prisoner is stressed by physical discomfort or worse, sleeplessness, noise, and uncertainty. There is at first only hostile interrogation, later one of the interrogators plays the role of prisoner's friend. When the prisoner breaks down, the 'friend' feeds in the necessary confession, or whatever change in behaviour is needed, and the prisoner adopts it. Children are often thoughtlessly exposed to extremes of fear and violence which they can neither endure nor escape, and adapt by learning to like such unpleasant feelings as the only way out of an intolerable situation. They experience this perversion as a sensation of excitement. In many towns the cinemas only keep going on a combination of horror, violence and sex. Lots of people enjoy the thrill of driving fast, many hunt for the pleasure of chasing and killing, though only a few will risk their lives to hunt a dangerous animal to really test their skill at shooting. The process of reversing the emotional reaction described above can also be used to help people. Leading someone to relive a disturbing experience, may induce a short period of intolerable stress, and at this time only there will be a response to suggestions about taking the situation in a new way. This is brainwashing in reverse. Another method is to gradually weaken the adverse conditioned reflex, by repeated use of the Watch Exercise.

Emotional disturbance is much more common than tolerant positive emotions. A good way of recognizing the disturbed state is by the feeling of intolerance that goes with it. Either the person cannot bear the situation he is in—and must escape from it, or he feels comfortable, but is critical of the state of mind, or behaviour of other people, or things. Either way it's turned, the feeling is intolerant. In the first instance it was directed inward—introverted as it is called, in the second instance it was outward on to others—that is, extroverted. But the main thing to remember is that the same emotion was in both. People tend to be predominately introverted, or predominately extroverted, but of course everyone can react both ways, and they often do not understand what is going on when they react in their less habitual way. They do not see that emotional response as the same, but directed in the opposite way. Extroversion is a state where the feeling of reality is experienced as being mainly outside the individual. Events therefore appear to happen through external causes. 'You are making me angry because . . .', 'I will never be happy unless . . .', 'Because I am now . . . , my cup is full', . . . are all the thoughts of an extrovert. They show no awareness of his inner world. Introversion occurs when the inner world of the personal self is more real than the external world. 'I wish I could make them understand how I feel.' 'I feel uncomfortable in this crowd.' 'I don't want to know anything about this', are all examples of an introverted way of taking life. Neither position gives a true picture. To experience life without distortion, a person should value the events of the inner world, and the external world equally, and be able to alter the balance as required by the occasion. Each should be treated with detachment, and even a touch of scepticism, so that consciousness of self is not lost in either extreme, nor is valuation of one world distorted by the valuation of the other. So, with this in mind, one can go on to the disturbances that occur in the three tolerant types of feeling, which, just like the intolerant ones, can also be directed in or out.

There are three ways in which a normal tolerant emotion can be disturbed. There can be none, too much, or the opposite. The disturbance can proceed each way, with varying intensity and along more than one way at a time. Two or more main forms of emotion can be disturbed together at the same time, and one can turn into another. For example, rejection and violence going on together produce hate; depression often is associated with a sense of being lonely. This may sound confusing—it is. Human beings are very mixed up emotionally. But, as a clear explanation of the range and types of human emotions cannot be given without apparently solidifying and simplifying them, this dissection must be given first. Emotions are interchangeable and rapidly fluctuating states, especially the disturbed ones, which are much more complex than the positive ones—faith, hope and charity. Emotion is mental energy. It reacts with physical energy as will be discussed in the next chapter, but it does not behave like a mechanical force. It is more like electricity, in that it can be either positive or negative. The positive emotions conserve, and seem to produce mental energy, since they allow it to flow. The negative emotions produce physical reactions by disturbing normal functioning of the body, and therefore seem to produce energy, but actually they waste mental energy by blocking its flow. Their effect is to produce mental inertia, and physical disorder, which together make it difficult to alter a disturbed emotional state. Because of this, frequently experienced negative emotions becoming habitual, produce fixed reactions. The number of possible responses is infinite. Each human being is unique, but there is a pattern which all follow, and an outline of the possible variations follows.

No Faith

In this direction, there is loss of the sense of order, and of trust in the existence of an overall pattern. The personality becomes more unstable, and being unstable seeks stability. Now, there is no stability in the universe—there is order, but nothing stays still. Everything is on the move physically and mentally. So a person without faith is always seeking something he can never find. What is experienced with varying intensity in this search is fear. If it is mild, it just keeps the sufferer anxious and restless; if severe, the person may be paralysed, totally frightened of everyone, and everything. This anxiety is free floating fear, not attached to anything.

One of the ways of tolerating an excessive amount of generalized fear, is to fix it on to a situation, or object, which then becomes intensely frightening, but because it can be avoided makes normal life free from fear. A fixed fear is often called a phobia—from the Greek word for fear, to distinguish it from free floating fear or anxiety. Now there are innumerable phobias. You name it, someone's got it. But there are common ones which everyone has had, such as fear of the dark, heights, enclosed spaces, dying, spiders, snakes, meeting people—shyness is a mild phobia and so on. Now while the anxious person just feels frightened and may develop behaviour which is obviously fearful and also the physical consequences of long continued fear, the phobic person is not frightened. The only time he does feel fear, is when faced with meeting his phobia. So he develops behaviour designed to avoid coming into any form of contact with it. For instance, a person with a phobia about heights, will never go up the Tower of Pisa, or near the edge of a cliff, and, if forced to, will produce many reasons why he should not. If the pressure to encounter his phobia is kept up, the reasons producing for avoiding it will seem more and more unreasonable, though they will seem very sound to the phobic person. If the phobia is severe, and the need to face it inescapable, the reasons and behaviour resulting from this situation, may become so strange, as to seem mad to an observer who is not in the same trap, and does not understand what is happening. Sometimes, phobias become forgotten, and their only manifestation is the odd behaviour they produce. This may disturb the sufferer, because he has compulsive urges which he cannot disobey without great stress, to behave in a way which seems absurd or inconvenient. This class of behaviour is called an obsession. To understand most obsessions, it is only necessary to look for the fear behind it. For instance, a girl got upset because she was always washing her hands—so much so, that she could not work. She had a phobia of poisoning someone by causing contamination of their food. She was a cook. But she also had to nurse a cantankerous elderly father she hated. She had thought of poisoning him. The abnormal fear of such a dreadful action made her unable to face this, and her behaviour continued, though she stopped washing her hands. She eventually starved herself to death. The death certificate said Anorexia Nervosa. She had a lot of other phobias as well, so she did not have much chance.

The main way of protecting oneself from fear is—neither to endure it nor to fix it, but to manufacture a safe position to live from. This, like the phobias, can take any form, from a small piece of stone to a place—an attitude—a form of behaviour—laws, rules, religion—anything to impose a sense of order and safety which has been lost by lack of faith. The order may be imposed upon oneself, or on the environment, or on both. The intensity with which the protection is imposed, varies with the degree of loss of faith. It can extend from a mild tendency to produce order in the environment such as making a garden, or being tidy, or insisting on 'good' manners, or a special diet, to a rabid fanaticism which can insist on the death penalty for belonging to a certain class or race, or losing one's capacity for earning because one does not have the same beliefs as those who impose them. This way of dealing with anxiety is the way of the 'normal' man—the way of society.

The tendency to impose an organization—to classify, to make rules, stems from the feeling that there is no order, so that one must be manufactured. It is not a ready acceptance of natural laws which occurs in a state of faith, but the imposition of a makeshift order to protect the individual or group from the fear engendered by lack of perception of a universal order. This organizing tendency is so common, it is accepted as normal behaviour. Of course everyone experiences it, just as everyone is occasionally frightened. Institutions, like the armed forces, and the police, are products of no faith, being manufactured organizations with the aim to protect citizens from attack or crime, maintain order, and enforce the authority of government. A church protects a religious doctrine from alteration. All organizations have a protective role. It does not matter what the aim of an organization is, it protects an interest. Where anyone feels an interest is worth protection—there is fear of its destruction or alteration, and an organization is manufactured to perpetuate it. The urges to consolidate for ever, to render immortal, to resist the eternal change of the universe, are the products of no faith.

Too Much Faith

Too much faith confers a strong desire to believe. As an exaggeration of a positive feeling it is in the direction of good. People with excessive faith are so certain of their beliefs they commit themselves fully. They feel they are right and, so are fearless. Therefore they feel justified in judging others by their standards, and can be sanctimonious know-alls. If of a passive unstable nature, they tend to believe anything, be gullible, and easily swayed, changing opinions frequently as they come under this or that influence. If somewhat more stable but still passive, they become attached to an organization, person, or faith, in which they can believe passionately. They need the support of a dogma, and are true believers. They provide the followers, the body of the faithful of every organization. They are fans and fanatics. In the pure form of passive excess faith they do not wish to change anything, but to believe in something outside themselves, which they feel they can trust. They have not got the inner sense of partaking, which is conferred by real faith in a state of balance with the other emotions. Consequently they are extroverted as are all the people who suffer from an excess of any of the three positive forms of feeling. Another characteristic of such people is that they like to give themselves labels. Everyone who says, 'I am a conservative, a socialist, a communist, a catholic, a Plymouth brother, an atheist, or black panther'—who identifies himself, with any cause, career, organization, or group whatsoever, is under the influence of the negative emotion excessive faith.

Too much faith makes for an all or nothing type of reaction. If positive such a person is a 'yes' man, if negative a 'no' man. That is he tends to react in either of these two ways to each event in his life. In mild degrees this is common, and not of much significance. In extremes 'yes' men are fairly harmless, and usually find their niche supporting the self-esteem of a stronger character, in marriage or employment, or getting the feeling of having some power in the shelter of a committee; but 'no' men can be very obstructive if they gain a position of power.

In active people the drive of too much faith confers an excess of zeal, and may take the form of doing good works, of excessive care about what other people believe or do, in brief, of being self-righteous. Busybodies they are, though not of course to themselves, they feel they are right in whatever they do, or believe. They are nuisances in the main, though in excess, too much faith confers a rigidity, which may cause trouble if they encounter a similar person with opposite views, or make them trouble others if they are in a position of power. The emotional state being described is what leads to religious massacres, wars, and political persecution. Being 'Strong in the faith' is literally true. Such people become fanatics, for they have the terrible self-confidence given by the feeling that whatever they do is right.

Negative Faith

Since faith confers a sense of order and trust, negative faith confers its opposites, a sense of mistrust and disorder. The disorderly aspects are easy to summarize. Instead of doing good people who feel with negative faith tend to do bad, and create disturbance. In the extreme, they are people with criminal tendencies, and those who get satisfaction out of suffering, either of others or their own. They are sadists or masochists. They are rebellious by nature, often going out of their way to express their lack of conformity. This may be manifested as ambition to stand out from the rest of the community, to literal rebellion against the Government. But though the extreme forms are clearly distinguishable, the dogged non-cooperator who imposes his own disorderly way of reacting on any situation, or relationship, shows a subtler form of negative faith. He has a sort of built-in tendency to take things as they are not. These types may, if they succeed, win admiration as pioneers, or rugged individualists. If less dominant and succcessful, they just seem to be continuously gritty, or are uncooperative misfits. Often their uncompromising lack of cooperation, may be concealed under a compliant smoke screen. Behind a cheerful, winning, and often startling appearance, which they use to fascinate, lurks a steely will and formidable ability to obstruct opposition, and get their own way. The quality of not accepting things as they are is at the centre of the disorderly person's reaction. The degree of intensity of this negative emotion determines the persistence and strength of the individual's response, giving progressively more resistance, obstinacy and rejection of things as they are up to a person who will sacrifice their life just to rebel against life itself.

For the sake of clarity, disorder and mistrust, which are both guises that negative faith takes, are being described separately—but both are mixed in people with this form of intolerant feeling, though a few people react predominantly in one of these two ways. The people who distrust have a suspicious nature. They question other people's motives, and tend to conceal their own. They are sceptical by nature, and need everything proven before they can commit themselves. Such a person tends to be materialistic and scientific in outlook, but this is not the rule. Other examples of the large scale effects of negative faith leading to lack of trust, are wars, and preparations for wars, strikes and widespread absence of religious feeling. In connection with any group, such as a nation, trade union, or religious faith, it should be noted that a tendency to organize is a product of no faith. An effort being made to impose order, and therefore stability, so that various organizations are produced. The tendency to believe is a product of too much faith, hence adherence to a doctrine even when formulated by a person with negative faith, will attract a person with too much faith. Many people high up an organization's hierarchy are often sceptics, and see through the organization completely, but this is far from the position of the humble faithful who need the organization for support. This state of affairs occurs because the adaptations to produce security, are similar in form to the products of a feeling of too much security. At intense extremes of feeling the opposites merge, fear into security, pain into pleasure, violence into peace. At a more mundane level however the organization creaks on, because the sceptical organization man is held in his position by fear of the consequences of giving it up, while the true believer needs the organization to express his excess of faith. The person with negative faith, however, turns excessively against organization, suspicious of its motives, and disliking its power for ruling him. He dislikes authority other than his own. He is a natural anarchist. He may isolate himself from others, or may join an organization, but will try to use it for his own ends. For example, these are the people who work for, and lead, wild-cat strikes. They will never last long in an organization, because they are always disruptive. Even if they have a good case, and win it on one occasion, they are soon making a disturbance again, and eventually their more stable colleagues begin to ignore them, so they move elsewhere and start again. In general, they tend to form the militants in any organization, and much change comes through their activities, but they do not produce a smoothly running machine. Many people start off in life mainly as agitators full of negative faith, disruptors, trying to change things as they are—get worn down, by the natural resistance of the other types of people, and the natural inertia of humanity, and change their form of emotional reaction to too much faith, or no faith, and become believers or security minded organizers. Sometimes both these forms of emotion are evenly divided, sometimes all three, from the start of a person's life. There you have the militant, believing, fear-driven, persistent, self-willed man. Bound to go to the top of any organization. Too frightened to do anything to hazard his position, driven to change things where he can, believing that by making plans, organizing affairs, and planning success will be assured. Political parties select such people to represent them; businesses search for them, the services promote them, and churches venerate them. In the disorders of faith is the fuel for success in the social activities of man.

In discussing the external effects on civilization of the disorders of faith, we have moved away from the effect of negative faith on relationships between people. Here the combination of mistrust and non-acceptance of the other as he is—as a person—is particularly damaging. It is in the home, where personal relationships are closest, that the situation is clearest. Such parents tend to produce children with a personality prone to mental breakdown, particularly the one called schizophrenia. This is literally a split mind in ancient Greek. People who have the tendency to behave 'normally' some of the time, but under stress, or a shock, change into a bizarre behaviour which is incomprehensible to their relatives and attendants. Often, if enough trouble is taken to find out the thoughts and feelings of the sufferer from this condition, they will be seen to be expressing a defence against their environment in the only way which seems open to them, because of the disturbing nature of their home life. Schizophrenia runs in families, so in addition to the disturbing effect of parents upon their children which could account for this, there is also a physically inherited abnormality of the brain. Some schizophrenics spontaneously experience long periods of changes in their way of seeing things which are the same as those sometimes induced by hallucinating drugs (LSD, etc.) for a short time. This can be a blissful healing experience or not. The mental illness called schizophrenia is not fully understood. Under this general heading are almost certainly several different sorts of phenomena which tend to produce a similar type of behaviour. But clearly Negative Faith is the emotional disturbance which underlies it.

No Hope

A person in the emotional state of no hope lacks the energy given by knowing that all will be well. Inertia is not overcome and so predominates. Movements and body processes are slow. The sufferer sits about and cannot concentrate on his work and life. Anxiety and guiltiness over his shortcomings occupy his mind. Above all, he feels depressed, and sees no hope of changing his state. If the hopeless mood persists, his body becomes affected, his appetite goes, he loses weight, he gets constipated and feels exhausted. Sleep comes easily enough, but he wakes in the early hours plagued by his depressive negative thoughts, and the secondary fears, guilts, loneliness, and confusion of his condition. He feels cold, often sweats and develops a host of minor physical symptoms, which convince him he is suffering from a serious physical illness—often cancer. These secondary body symptoms can worry him more than the depression, and are mostly what make him go to his doctor. As well as the physical symptoms directly produced by the depression—a person who is depressed often develops a common illness which is not usually associated with depression, for example, pneumonia or a coronary thrombosis. Coupled with his depression, he becomes over-sensitive to normal stimuli—simple noises, for instance, affect him severely. A telephone bell is like being in a belfry, birds shriek outside, a gentle suggestion wounds like a severe reprimand. According to whether a person is active or passive, he will be suicidal or not, but his other emotional disturbances also influence what he experiences.

Psychiatrists classify depressions in various ways, but this is not of much importance. The essential emotional disorder is the state of No Hope. The apparent variation in the types is due to the seed and the soil; the type of person who becomes depressed, sex, age, external circumstances, and previous history. For example, a person who is also fearful becomes more so when depressed—he is said to have an Agitated Depression. Someone who, before they became depressed had an upsetting experience is said to have a Reactive Depression. If no depressing circumstances can be found, it is considered to come from within the personality—to be Endogenous, and so on. Classification is a human pastime, compensating for no faith.

Too Much Hope

Too little hope often alternates with too much hope. People subject to the disturbances of hope frequently have swings of mood from depression into overactivity with excessive optimism. If this is severe, the excess energy drives the mind very fast, and of course, also the body. Ideas flow so fast that communication becomes difficult, as speech cannot cope with the speed of mental activity. The sufferer raves disjointedly. His mood is usually cheerful, but it is a frustrating sort of state to be in. The attempts of those around to cope and restrain the maniac do irritate him, and such is the force of hope involved, that the resulting anger and violence are of gigantic proportions.

Excess hope can stimulate all the other disturbed emotions to be more strongly active, and has the same effect on the drives. One in particular—imagination—is worth more description. This is strongly stimulated, and fantasies proliferate abundantly. Fantasy may occupy the waking hours and become more real than physical reality. Touch with life may be lost, or the sufferer prefer the fantasy to reality. It is like being in a dream, or under drugs, continuously. In excess, this is a form of madness called paranoia. In combination with Negative Faith, considerable disturbance occurs, and this is common because children in a hostile constricting environment defend themselves by making life tolerable with imagination. It should be borne in mind that though some forms of insanity are being described, that all these processes go on in everyone without any exceptions. There are lots of awful people who do not find life too much for them, unlike the more gentle weaker people, of far greater perception, who break down, or go mad. Those who are strong, survive in life by making it unpleasant for others, enforcing their screwy opinions on the weak. The more rabid of them may occupy public positions, which portray their tendencies—the torture squad of the secret police is an example, and many milder examples of this type of person occupy respected official positions in the community—but this type of behaviour is common in the home. It is called 'bringing up children'. It is actually the imposition of fantasy upon the defenceless young. It goes on everywhere. Every parent has done it. See how you do it, too. Child battering is a gross example of this sort of behaviour, and is commoner than realized.

Negative Hope

Some of the energy for the destructive power of the imagination comes from the reversal of hope. Hope builds up, Negative Hope destroys. It provides the energy for violence. Because this is a short simple section, its effect is not to be underrated. It is universal, and is one of the great disruptive forces of man. War destroys, but mental violence deforms man. This, too, is one of the cottage industries of man. Children either learn to be violent from their parents, or are cowed by their parents' violence, so that they form too weak a personality dominated by one or several of the types of negative emotion now being described. A common reaction is for the child to have violent feelings towards the parent in response to those turned upon them. But since they are too small to express it successfully they are bottled up and forgotten. This suppression constrains the parent-child bond into an unnatural and uneasy dependent relationship. It may only be a source of an unnatural tension, but may produce guilt, violence, depression, and often physical symptoms.

No Charity

Intellectually, words are descriptive labels for ideas, things, and states of feeling, In poetry, words can also be used as musical sounds, and combining both these aspects is a difficult art. But this book is prose. In understanding prose describing ideas and feelings, abstract states not physical things, one must always be trying to see the meaning behind the label. For each label does have a special meaning for the reader, so if you have a feeling that charity is what is given to the poor, like the Charity Commissioners who dole out blankets and coal, and money at Christmas, put that out your mind. Instead of Charity, love could have been used as it is commonly used to label the feeling now being described, but the meaning of love contains more than charity and will be used later in Chapter 8.

Facing life with charity allows giving what is needed in any situation—of uniting with it effectively. Charity is not forceful. It is a way of taking life. Without charity there is a sense of lack of need for giving, for union, with people, things and places. People lacking charity are dependent upon these three to fill their sense of emptiness. They go through life seeking charity, attaching themselves to others, to furniture, districts, houses, money, so that they are unable to conceive living without them, and become depressed if forced to. If the dependency is great, the person is obviously inadequate to live except in a very sheltered way with someone to prop them up all the time. They often find the solution is not to leave home, or to marry another dependent person, so they can prop each other up, by each supplying the other's need. If forced to leave home, or when not in a dependent relationship to someone or something else, they often obtain satisfaction by joining an organization. The dependent are very gregarious. The person without enough love feels lonely. Much peculiar behaviour, and much sexual relationship, occurs between people whose only reason for them is that they are lonely. This is a poor reason for getting married. It leads to many marriages breaking up when the partner who is not dependent gets fed up. A hazard of dependency found mainly in women, is that they transfer the source of satisfaction from their husband to their children, particularly if sex does not attract them, for they cannot obtain satisfaction when the children, who they have been feeding on all their lives, and not giving to, go away, as they get repelled into doing. When this happens these mothers are filled with a sense of deep loss. Their husbands have found other interests. They feel useless and often get depressed, because there is no hope of a way out. Some, however, adapt by taking on an alternative role, and take a job, do good works, play bridge, or get another man. These have been called displacement activities. The principle is that if you cannot endure a situation, or change it, you can manufacture another more pleasant situation as an alternative to live from. Women are not the only ones who have this problem. The dependent man often transfers his dependency to his job. Or if this does not satisfy him, to a hobby, committee, or social work. On reaching middle age he finds he has got as far as he can in that field. There are no more prospects for him—he has reached his full capacity—and there is no more to do than go on repeating what he is the master of. This can come as a shock, and is unsettling and depressing. Lacking a close attachment with his wife and children, he looks around for a substitute. If he cannot change his occupation, he may become a hazard to his female employees, or fall for any unattached woman who wants such a relationship. Alternatively, if too inhibited sexually by his situation or morals, he will develop a nervous breakdown, or physical illness, such as a coronary thrombosis. All these reactions are very common hazards of the forties and fifties.

People in a state of No Charity, conserve their depleted emotional stores. If they give out too much they feel more lonely, inadequate and dependent, so they hold on to their energy exclusively, and they live with little attention or involvement, and tend to be lazy and careless. The phrase 'I couldn't care less' is a typical example of this emotional state.

Too Much Charity

The idea of there being an excess of charity is hard to conceive—especially to the sentimental. But you can have too much of a good thing. If you care too much for something you can't do without it. You become addicted to it. If there is too much giving to the object of one's attention, nothing else is taken in, and the ability to respond to other stimuli is lost. There is total absorption of attention, so there will be over-specialization if this state is continued too long. In a state of excess charity, a person will give themselves totally to another person or organization, or object, or habit—a willing slave, who often does not know he is a slave, especially if he has a tendency to excess faith or no faith. The problem of addiction is not confined to drugs, drink, smoking, the slow killers which also induce a chemical dependency, but simply being alive is a form of addiction; we have a tendency to become addicted to any life activity, and therefore dependent upon it. Why does everyone, at least at sometime of their lives, fear death? Because they are addicted to life. Apart from this universal generalized addiction, there are an infinite number of addictions to all aspects of life; again, if you name it someone has it. People tend to regard addiction as abnormal, but it is only the unusual and lethal ones that produce interest. The normal addictions tend to pass unnoticed because these are so familiar. Let's mention a few common addictions—playing games, keeping pets, eating, sex, power, movement and money. If one likes money too much, one can store it up, and be mean about it, and so become a miser. See your addiction—what is precious to you? What can't you do without? You're addicted to it.

Negative Charity

The opposites of giving and joining-with are rejection and repulsion. Negative charity is a state of not giving, of meanness. Love and hate are usually considered opposites—so, since charity is the word being used in this section for what is commonly called love, an obvious substitution would be to call charity and hate opposites. But hate is not the simple opposite of charity. It is a mixed emotion consisting of rejection and violence in equal proportions. Similarly, jealousy is a mixture of fear and violence. Because you fear someone's attributes might be better, or more successful, than your own, you feel violent towards him, and the resulting mixture is experienced as jealousy. Envy is partly desire to be like, or have the same as another person, and the other part of this mixed emotion is rejection. Envy is a passive state, jealousy is much more like hate—it is active. That is why its second portion is violence. Rejecting someone as a person, feeling repulsed by someone or something, and being mean are clear enough examples of the state of negative charity. It is more difficult to see how self-love is also the same disturbance. The characteristic of charity is that it involves a consideration of others, not primarily oneself. In order to be charitable one has to give the situation or person one is involved with what they need, not what 'I' need.

One has to be entirely unselfish in order to be charitable. Charity involves the same consideration and affirmation of the other as oneself. But to place oneself in any way before others is not charity, it is self-love; that is, preferring the needs of oneself to those of others, pushing oneself forward, valuing oneself more than others, and taking pleasure in one's abilities when they are greater than others which is pride. Everyone is different, we all have different gifts or attributes, with which we are born. In some ways we are more skilful or intelligent, or quicker than others. But this does not mean we are superior. For example, they may be more skilful, and quicker in other ways; they may have more understanding and be far more perceptive emotionally. As people we are equal, all else is pride and vanity. Vanity is taking pride in imaginary attributes which we have not got. A typical example of vanity is the pleasure humans take in trying to seem beautiful, dressing themselves up, painting, curling, scenting, to appear to be what they are not. Vanity is taking pride in fantasy. A less obvious form of vanity is the playing of the role of being unselfish, of putting oneself last, of self-denial, which in extremes can take the form of self-punishment, even torture, in the delusion that in this adversity there is virtue. That idea is rubbish. It is only one part of the personality based on self-love taking pride, in tormenting the animal side, because of its wholly reasonable and natural appetites. Though this form of self-love is not common, the feeling of shame when pride and vanity are shown up, is. But above all, self-love is the mainspring of the personality, an enormous lopsided over-development which disturbs everyone's balance. Say 'I', and there is self-love. It is necessary to have some in order to exist among other human beings who are dominated by it, but it gives a false sense of individuality, and a false motivation of life which is of enormous importance. In order to escape from self-love, one has to see how much and what parts of one's life are motivated by it, and then struggle to transform the motivation into charity. This involves for everyone an, at first, strange sensation of selflessness. Instead of the old sense of I, saying 'I think this' or 'I am feeling that', it is as if 'I' was being thought by something outside one's personality. To put it another way, one gets outside one's thoughts and feelings and observes them. There is a sense of 'I' but a different and more impersonal one—one is no longer one's thoughts and feelings.

People can protect themselves from suffering the state of negative charity by not giving. But it is not possible to get without giving. Living is a dynamic process. Such people don't find it easy to give anything away, they don't spare much time on others, above all they don't give in sex. They may be able to achieve orgasm but the emotional relationship in sex is lacking in that quality of mutual sympathy which brings that act to perfection. They are indifferent to others, because they can only consider themselves. They are selfish, and therefore need their self-esteem. While many people whose selfishness is outwardly turned will spend much energy in ensuring that their requirements are met, some people meet the problem of not giving by conserving their energy excessively. They are solitary, cut off, and cold.

The aim of this chapter has been to show the results of feeling too much or too little, or the opposite of the three main emotions. The situation is summarized in the chart on page 63 where the attitudes these disturbed emotions produce are listed. Everyone has them at one time or another. It is not possible to respond rightly to certain situations without experiencing them. It is not a question of good or bad feelings, of primitive or negative responses. That is over-simple —but of holding a state of balance—in which neither Faith, Hope nor Love is felt too much, but all combine to produce an appropriate response. When this is done, there is no disturbance which can upset the body. When this is not so, the unpleasant emotions disturb its functions and produce a physical reaction. Try to find out which form of imbalance is most common for you, and therefore what transformation it would be best to make.

Suppose you now know which intolerant emotions are your main tendency, then their positive emotion is the one unto which you should try to change your habitual reaction, using the watch exercise as described in Chapter 8 if you have difficulty.

In making any decision, or performing any action, try to make sure your emotional state is tolerant, or positive, and that there are equal values of hope, faith, and charity brought to bear on the event. If this is done you will disturb neither others, yourself, nor the world you live in.

FAITH	*No Faith* There is no sense of order. Therefore there is: No Stability, &/or Free fear—Anxiety, or Fixed fear—Phobias, or Obsessions, or The wish to impose order and security, or The tendency to organize.	*Too Much Faith* There is an excessive sense of order. Therefore there is: Too much trusting, &/or Believing, or Rigidity, or Doing 'Good' Works, or Certainty, or Self-righteousness, or Judging others.	*Negative Faith* There is a sense of disorder. Therefore there is: Mistrust, &/or Disbelief, or Rebellion, or Doing 'Bad' Works, or Schizophrenia, (intrusion of disorder).
HOPE	*No Hope* There is no hope. Therefore there is: Depression &/or No energy, or Guilt.	*Too Much Hope* There is excessive energy and expansion. Therefore there is: Excess mental activity, &/or Excess imagination, or Fantasy, or Delusions (Paranoia), or Mania.	*Negative Hope* The energy of the mind is destructive. Therefore there is: Violence, & /or Destruction.
CHARITY	*No Charity* There is a sense of lacking—of wanting—of not caring. Therefore there is: Dependency (on people, things, places), &/or a Feeling of Inadequacy, or Loneliness, or Indifference, or Carelessness, or Laziness.	*Too Much Charity* There is excessive commitment. Therefore there is: Excessive involvement in everything and life, &/or Identification with roles, people, etc., or Overspecialization, or Addiction, or Desire, or Tendency to collect.	*Negative Charity* There is no ability to unite with and care for others. Therefore there is: Rejection, &/or Repulsion, or Self love and selfishness, or Pride / Vanity } Shame, or Meanness, or Inability to 'give'.

Attitudes Resulting from the Emotional Disturbances

Find the emotional disturbances you have—often more than one.
Some disturbed emotions are combinations:

Worry is fear + involvement (No Faith + Too Much Charity)
Hate is rejection + violence (Negative Charity + Negative Hope)
Jealousy is fear + violence (No Faith + Negative Hope)
Envy is desire + rejection (Too much Charity + Negative Charity)

The disturbed emotions may be:

Extroverted—outwardly directed on to others, and/or,
Introverted—inwardly directed on to oneself.

Mental change begins with the transformation of the disturbed, or intolerant, emotions into the positive ones—Faith, Hope and Charity.

6

Disorders of Mind and Body

In the previous chapter the disorders of the mind produced by disturbed emotions have been described. In this chapter the reaction between the body and the mind is considered. Disease arises as much from the mind as from the body—each influences the other equally. A disturbed physical body produces alterations in the function of the mind, and a disturbed mind distorts the body. But, because disturbed emotions are commoner than inherited faults, most, perhaps as much as three-quarters, of human illness is produced by mental disturbances. Often it is easy to see how this occurs, sometimes difficult. There may be an immediate relationship between mind and body or a delayed one. For instance, smoking causes, or at any rate more smokers develop, cancer of the lung, and coronary thromboses, than people who do not smoke. These are delayed effects of being a habitual cigarette smoker. The immediate effects are a chemical bronchitis and nicotine poisoning. Another example is alcoholism which produces fibrosis of the liver and its eventual failure assisted by the deficient diet which alcoholics eat. Alcohol has, also, an immediate effect on the liver, heart, brain and kidneys. It poisons the cells, but these effects, like those of other drugs of addiction, are mostly reversible unless the amounts taken are very high, when they may kill. Other drugs, such as morphia, and heroin, are so addictive and stupefying that the addict ends up in a starved, dopey state with infections from the injections he gives himself, rather than face the awful withdrawal symptoms. He dies from a combination of the immediate and delayed effects. Marihuana, or Pot, if taken regularly, builds up in the body, and produces a state of stupefaction, but it is not particularly addictive, no more than alcohol or smoking, and its addicts being more peaceable than alcoholics, are therefore less accident prone. To date, there is no good evidence that the mescaline-lysergic acid group of drugs are dangerously addictive, though their effects, just like alcohol, can be disastrous in disturbed people, many of whom use alcohol, which is at present more socially acceptable, to escape from the reality of living.

Addictions to psychological habits and attitudes can also have long-term physical effects on the body depending upon their intensities, and the length of time they are indulged in. For instance, some passive people would rather endure than resolve the situations they find difficult, and often get indigestion. If they do happen to have real difficulties to cope with, and these states go on, they may develop a duodenal ulcer. Exactly how this happens does not concern us here. It is the 'why' that is more important. It is the effect of the disturbed emotional states on the body that matters. The reactions between the animal and human sides of a person, are not the reactions between mind and body, both the former take place in the mind, but there can be conflicts between them. These produce disturbed emotional states and upset the functions of the body. All diseases are psychosomatic, for man is a psychosomatic organism. Disturbances of the mind affect the body, disturbances of the body affect the mind. The effects of the disturbances in each compartment produce secondary influences in the other compartment. It is like an echo going on and on and on, thrown back from one reflecting surface to another, until inertia wears down the initial force. A simple way of looking at it is to think of diseases as made up of the product of mind and body in different amounts—like a spectrum made up of light shining through two different coloured wedges of glass placed together to make an oblong. One wedge represents mind, the other body.

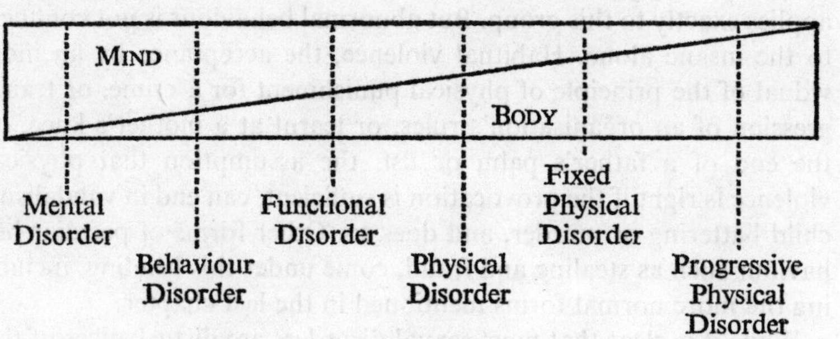

According to where the light strikes the long sides, a gradation from one colour into the other is produced. This is only a hypothetical model. The reality of the reaction is quite different. I do not know how it happens, I could make some guesses, but it really does not matter how it does take place. What is important is to be aware that it does happen in the manner just discussed, which can provide a working hypothesis for action, and be modified if necessary. The action is the basis for living, and it is how we live that is important, not how physical changes come about. Now, if the spectrum is split up into parts, starting from the bit which is practically entirely mental, and moving from left to right into the part which is practically all physical body, there are a number of different types of human disorder which can be described. These blend imperceptibly into each other.

There are *mental disorders* which hardly affect the body at all, or may be determined by some small inherited defect. This does not mean that the results cannot be fatal. Many people impulsively kill themselves when frustrated, or out of shame, when there is no physical disorder present at all. This does not mean that seriously depressed people do not have an inherited, or acquired physical body illness which makes them depressed. Nor does it exclude a purely emotional depressive state from lack of hope, affecting the body, and producing physical changes in it. All these three things happen, and would occupy different parts of the spectrum farther to the right of the mainly mental disorder. Depression is not the only mental disturbance that behaves in this way. All the other ones do.

The next group of disorders are those of *behaviour*. Here the field is not only in the mind but also in action. Of course, these two groups blend into each other. Mental disorders are often described by the behaviour they produce, and what has been said about the last group applies exactly to this group. But abnormal behaviour is not confined to the insane alone. Habitual violence, the acceptance by an individual of the principle of physical punishment for a crime, or transgression of an organisation's rules, or learnt at a mother's knee, or the end of a father's palm or fist, the assumption that physical violence is right if the provocation is sufficient, can end in vandalism, child battering or murder, and does so. Other forms of peculiar behaviour such as stealing and fraud, come under this heading, including the more normal forms mentioned in the last chapter.

While it is clear that most sexual disorders are disturbances of the mind acted out in behaviour and fluctuate between these two groups, producing emotional tensions, such as fear and depression, some may have a physical basis in temporary hormonal disturbances which occurred when imprinting was going on in early childhood. Examples of these are homosexuality and transvestism. These disorders also need a disturbed relationship with the parent of the opposite sex of the type already described in order to develop. But though apparently behavioural only, this physical basis at the level of imprinting is probably why, once established by active practice after puberty, they are so seldom changed.

Still moving from left to right in the spectrum comes the *functional disorders* where the working of the body is disturbed. These are entirely reversible disturbances of function such as a racing heart, sweating, and shaking, wheezing, or not digesting food. They are mostly intermittent. But sometimes if the body's reaction is severe, or the emotional upset is considerable, or continuous, death can result, or physical disease develop. For example, people have died of grief or shock, and young people sometimes die of severe asthma. In this group come the conditions usually described in medical textbooks as psychosomatic disorders. Asthma is a good example. This has a large inherited element. In some people this is predominant and they come in the next group, the reversible physical disorders, or even the one after that, the fixed physical disorders which are not reversible. But usually asthma is precipitated by an emotional disturbance, and is a functional disorder. The infections which are associated with it, and often precipitate attacks, because they aggravate an already irritable set of bronchial tubes, are frequent, because asthma makes the lungs more easily infected. But what about the allergic element? That is also inherited, is associated with the tendency to wheeze, and behaves in exactly the same way. Where the word asthma is used, just say 'asthma and allergy'—they go hand in hand. One is more dominant than the other in different people, and at different ages. In some people asthma is a way of behaving. They use that wheeze to obtain sympathy, or as a warning they are being stressed beyond their limits, or as a means of excusing themselves from doing something they find unpleasant. To them, asthma is a way of life, learnt just as a child learns to form a personality as described in Chapter 4 by imprinting and conditioning. All teachers will know of children who wheeze as soon as things get difficult, and have to go home. All doctors, and nurses, know of patients who start up wheezing as soon as they enter the ward. Asthma has been described in detail, not because there is anything unusual about it, but because it is a typical example of a psychosomatic disorder. It has an inherited physical side, and a mental side. It can be, in any one person, at the same time, or at different times and ages, a behavioural, functional, reversible physical or fixed physical disorder, and this holds for all the other examples of this special type of disorder, because the principle is true of all illnesses.

After functional disorders come the *reversible physical disorders*. Typical of these are infections, which produce an illness that may have a scar, but when healed leave a normal body free of disease—wounds and fractures are of a similar nature. The physical element is easy to see here. The mental factor is less prominent. No one exposed to an overwhelming dose of an infecting oganism, will fail to get this disease, but disturbed emotional states are known to lower resistance to infection, and one eminent child psychiatrist (Melanie Klein) said that no child got an infection without a preceding emotional upset. That is an exaggeration, for all children exposed to an overwhelming infection will become ill. The psychological factor in accidents and wounds due to fighting is more obvious. It takes carelessness to be involved in most accidents, but of course not always. Sometimes innocent passengers or bystanders are involved. Nervous indigestion is a functional disorder. If it goes on long and severely enough, an ulcer forms. This can heal, mainly as a result of putting the patient to bed, assisted by other forms of medical treatment. The putting to bed solves the patient's problems by temporarily removing him from them. This is just what suits the passive personality who gets ulcers. Ulcers also run strongly in families, and that is the inherited physical element. When he gets back into circulation again with the ulcer healed, it soon recurs, because the same difficulties are encountered again, and so it usually goes on healing and breaking down, until the duodenum is so scarred up that it begins to bleed frequently, or blocks up the outlet to the stomach; the stages of fixed and progressive physical disorders are entered. Death or operation, or both, are the only possibilities open now. Operations for peptic ulcer which remove a bit of the stomach or its nerve supply, when done for relief of pain, all result in some degree of interference with the ability to absorb food. Most people lose weight after these operations, and some get seriously starved. There are other more unpleasant consequences, but these only occur in about 10 per cent of the sufferers. It seems a pity that so many people have to be so mutilated to escape from a pain which in many of them could be prevented by their changing their attitudes before a hole in the stomach had formed.

To make the point clear, take the example of a man who has a family history of indigestion, or ulcers. He is over-conscientious, becomes angry easily, and finds his relationship with his wife and children difficult. He works hard, and thinks his mates lazy, but in spite of his industry—probably because he is quarrelsome, promotion eludes him. Because of this, and because his wife's attention seems occupied with the children, for she finds him too difficult, he feels lonely and neglected. This is the period of mental disturbance alone. His wife thinks he does not earn enough, and is impossible. They live in relative poverty, and quarrel often. He smokes and drinks too much. This is the period of behaviour disorder. After a few years of this life he gets indigestion and consults his doctor. A stomach X-ray shows nothing wrong. His doctor tells him it's nervous indigestion and he must 'pull himself together'. The situation and symptoms continue, partially relieved by a diet and medicines. This is the period of functional disorder. He falls seriously behind with hire-purchase commitments, and the television set is removed. The resulting domestic tension produces an increase in his symptoms, and four years after the onset of his symptoms a second X-ray shows a definite ulcer. His doctor, more sympathetic now, puts him off work, intensifies his treatment and tells him he 'must learn to live with his ulcer'. He gets better in a few weeks and returns to work. But soon his symptoms return. He is off work frequently. Three years later his wife leaves him. He drinks a lot, his ulcer perforates, and is sewn up in hospital. This is the stage of physical disorder. He lives in digs, having casual relations with women, smoking heavily, drinking intermittently, and eating irregular meals. After another five years he takes Aspirin for a hangover, and this precipitates a bleed from his ulcer. On this occasion the X-ray shows a deformed and scarred duodenum. The awful warnings at the hospital frighten him into avoiding Aspirin, and induce a relative temperance. Fibrosis has begun. He is in the stage of permanent physical disorder, and entering the progressive phase. The almost constant pain from his ulcer makes him even more irritable, and depresses him. He loses his job. He is getting older, past fifty now, and the emotional fires begin to die down. He cannot afford to drink and smoke so much. The process slows and it is another ten years before his stomach outlet scars up completely, and he begins vomiting. An operation is now essential to relieve the situation. It would have been better to do one before.

But people who live like him always do badly and that put his medical advisers off this course. In his case, he was lucky, and did not get any of the complications of this operation. But he again lost his job, and is too old now to get another. Medical treatment by diet, alkalis and drugs has helped to keep him more comfortable during his sufferings, but has not made any difference to the outcome. If he had been told his approach to life needed changing, and what he should do about it, and how this affected his stomach, his life might have been different. At least he would have had a chance.

This imaginary man with a duodenal ulcer has shown that an illness can manifest in all the divisions of the spectrum and has jumped ahead a little by introducing further categories, the fixed, irreversible stage which never heals, the fixed physical disorders and the progressive physical disorders which go on, and on relentlessly, until the patient dies of the disease.

In the *fixed physical disorders* the mental element is less obviously active, and in fact in many it may be absent as a cause, or manifest only as a secondary effect of the physical disorder on the mind, such as the irritability and depression produced by severe pain, or the disturbances of memory and personality that occur in some dietary deficiencies. Inherited mental disorders, gland and enzyme deficiencies are also examples of this group, which, once established, do not in themselves progress, though their effects can be fatal if not corrected.

In the *progressive group* the mental side is imperceptible, except in the past. Even if it is altered, the progressive process will go on, like the scarring up of the ulcer. There are secondary effects upon the mind, as in the fixed group, but these are less prominent except in the early stages. Typical examples of these are cancers and progressive blood diseases, like leukaemia. On the other hand, cancer of the lung is an indirect effect of the addiction to tobacco, and is therefore caused by an emotional disturbance. Evidence is also accumulating that, in an as yet unknown way, the type of person one is, influences the diseases one gets, even if it is a progressive physical one. For instance, more women with depressive tendencies get cancer of the womb than those who are cheerful. Men with striving restless personalities are more liable to get coronary thrombosis, than those who are placid and non-competitive. So the emotions influence atheroma, which is also a slowly progressive physical disorder. But coronaries frequently occur after emotional disturbances, so some of these are functional disorders of the already diseased arteries of the heart.

One of the difficulties in the way of clear thinking is the system of medicine dominant in the world today. This is based on the examination of broken-down bodies, from which an idea of the way they did so is arrived at through studying the abnormal chemical and physical processes involved, as well as their normal functions. Treatment consists of interfering with the disordered processes by replacement of lost chemicals, or blocking the disease processes with other chemicals foreign to the body, or by operations to do the same sort of thing. The idea that the mind could influence the body, only came to be grafted on to the system long after it had been well established. Consequently, doctors seem to regard the mind as only a physical and chemical process situated in the brain which can break down just like the rest of the body. They think all the emotions and feelings could, if only we knew enough, be explained in terms of physics and chemistry. Perhaps an analogy would make this clearer. A doctor is like a garage mechanic who repairs broken-down cars, using his knowledge of how they are made (anatomy), how they run (physiology) and the ways in which they break down (pathology). He uses the techniques of a history of the symptoms, the physical signs, and special tests to make a diagnosis, and then supplies the deficiency, refashions the broken part, or replaces it according to what is needed. He does not bother about the effect the driver has on the car, the failures of maintenance, the accidents, and so on. Or if he does think about it, makes the assumption that the driver is another machine which functions exactly like the car. The point is that the driver is not the same sort of machine as a car. The driver (the mind) is of a different nature altogether from the car (the body). The garage mechanic doctor does excellent work, and the system appears to work well as long as its limitations are accepted. It is based on the assumption that the defect in the car is an end in itself. That the machine is productive of symptoms, signs, disorders and diseases. It is taking the view that the functions of sense organs, brain and nervous system are only productive, which they are to a certain extent, and entirely ignoring the possibility that they can be also protective, and act as filters, preventing our consciousness from having to deal with more than it can bear, or is suitable for life on earth. The productive side of the nervous system is the response of the body and mind to the impressions recorded by various sense organs. These are confined to a few octaves of sound waves, a little more than an octave of light waves, and the effects of touch, pressure and gravity. There is so much, so incredibly much more, going on about us, of which we are not aware. When one starts to ponder over what we do not perceive, the sense based mind starts to boggle, probably quite rightly, for it was not designed for such perceptions. Nevertheless, man has the possibility of perceiving more than his brain can analyse. Think of the ultra sound he cannot hear, perhaps just as well because it can have a damaging effect on animal tissues. The light waves we cannot see, the ions, electrical waves, magnetic fields and so on, that are not perceptible to us. These are some of the physical surroundings that our sense organs cut us off from. We only know about them through instruments. There are also the thoughts, perceptions, ideas and feelings, from which our limiting brains cut us off—all our memory, all knowledge. What comes through is a pathetic trickle. Yet we love the brain, and are so proud of its achievements, for self-love is its fuel. We hold to the theory that the chemistry of the body produces our thoughts, feelings, and sensations, whereas actually it prevents us from perceiving an enormous amount, and distorts what we do see by its own interference in the process of perception.

The function of the brain as an excluding filter of perception, of course, does not stop it also being a producing organ of its own. All living things have their contribution to make. But it is important not to take a one-sided view, and treat the brain only as a mind-producing organ. To do so makes the difficulty of understanding disease inherent in scientific medicine. It is one-sided. A point of view which takes both the functions of the brain into consideration is needed, and this has been described in this chapter. This allows the needs of a sick person to be understood, and supplied with more precision and less harm. By allowing the sufferer to understand why his disease came about, it helps him to learn how he can prevent its recurrence.

It is the possibility of preventing a lot of physical disease which makes the approach described here so important. Because everyone gets emotionally disturbed at times, and some people are continually so most of their lives, relatively little disease is caused by physical disturbances such as inherited genetic disorders, and exposure to various physical factors such as poisons, germs, rays, climate, ions, sound and so on. At least three-quarters of all disease is caused by psychological disturbance. In fact, there is not much doubt that if all disease was re-examined from this point of view, the proportion would be found higher, say, 85 per cent.

It is easy to say that if the money spent on developing the physical types of treatment which so expensively produce, and maintain, invalids in precarious ill health a little longer than they would otherwise have lived—for example, the coronary care, renal, neurological and cardiac surgery units that are springing up all over the world, were spent on publicity in persuading people that the contents of this chapter were true, that there would be less disease. It is true, but addicts won't be persuaded to change. In spite of publicity, which has by now informed everyone in the world who reads that smoking cigarettes kills, their sales go up. The inertia of the Won't Factor is very strong. It is too much for most people, but some individuals may be persuaded to change themselves. One may not be able to change world events as an individual—but an individual can change his personal inner world.

7

Dreams and Psychic Phenomena

EVERYONE dreams, but a dream is a unique event in the dreamer's inner world. Dreams occur when the filter action of the brain is dulled in sleep, and are easily forgotten during its productive phase in the daytime when the outer personality is dominant. They occur in periods of sleep which are lighter than usual, and characterized by rapid eye movements.

No person's dreams are exactly the same as another's. Always, the individual's uniqueness remains unchallenged. However, all over the world, in different civilizations and times, people have the same sort of dreams. The falling dream, being chased, the wise old woman or man, the island rising out of the sea, the four-square garden, the fountain, flying, and so on.

Dreams are one of the ways in which the subconscious mind speaks to the individual. Sometimes dreams are just superficial jumbles made up of the flotsam and jetsam of everyday life, but often they are compensatory. A person on a revolting diet will dream of eating a banquet, a sex-starved person of having sexual intercourse. If a person is stopped dreaming through being woken as soon as he begins, by someone watching for the rapid eye movements, he soon starts to break down mentally. This fact is made use of in brain-washing. So the compensatory function of dreams is important, even though nothing is recalled by the conscious mind on waking. Dreams can also be studied by willing oneself to wake up just after the dream, and to write it down. Only a few notes are needed to allow a full recollection of the dream. Some people find this practice easy, and soon do not need the notes. They can recall their dreams on waking. In fact, after learning about interpretation, and some practice, it is possible to wake sufficiently to make a conscious interpretation of the dream symbols during the dream, understand its message and remember it on waking. This is easiest early in the morning just after waking. Then one can drift in and out of dreams, and even dream while awake.

After some experience it is clear that there are big dreams and little dreams. The big dreams are in colour and their contents are unusual in some way. Usually their chief characteristic is that they have never been seen before by the dreamer. They have an out of this world quality. Sometimes a big dream will be heralded by a voice from nowhere speaking to the dreamer. Such dreams have a message which can be useful if their meaning is understood. One of the strange things about people is how they laugh at dreams. 'Funny,' they'll say, 'I dreamt I was cutting the wife's throat the other night . . . absurd, isn' it.' They are only too ready to use the defence of making a joke about something they don't want to realize. No product of the mind is meaningless, though it may be incomprehensible at the time. One of the strange things about dreams is that they are free of the normal passage of time, typical of the waking state in the physical world. The present, past, and future are often mixed up in them. It is also true that their messages often cut right to the bone. Though brutally true, what they have to communicate is often put with a sense of humour. For instance, a woman who was a great dreamer, was having psychotherapy. She had made good progress simply by discussing and interpreting the dreams. More than once when a mistake was made, she would dream of her doctor wearing a dunce's cap, or standing in the corner. When the mistake was corrected, she would dream of him in a more favourable situation, as a master chef, for instance.

Dreams use the language of symbolism. Each person or thing in a dream represents a part of the personality, or a person in oneself. A house or a city represents the whole of one's mind; upper or lower parts of these signify thought or the instincts; slums or palaces, bad or good parts. If there are three stories, intellect, emotions and instincts are being symbolized. Plants, furniture, and clothes indicate attitudes and ways of taking things. Light signifies the conscious side, dark the unknown side of oneself. An animal represents either a basic characteristic, or an instinctive trait. In a man, a woman represents his emotional side. In a woman, a man portrays the masculine, thinking side. The age of a person represents an older or younger stage of one's life, or in one's mental growth. Birds or aeroplanes signify thoughts; water or fluids, such as petrol and the sea, emotions. Earthy substances such as clay, brick or stone, mean material aspects of the logical and instinctive mind. Fire or explosions can mean outbursts of emotional energy. Light and air signify consciousness, understanding and spiritual matters. Parents in dreams, or old people, may represent the accepted and acquired traits one has in oneself, which are those of the person dreamt about, or they may mean older parts of oneself. If they are kings or queens they refer to ruling parts of one's mind, worldly aspects usually. The state of health of the people in dreams has the same significance for the corresponding part of one's personality. Death psychologically means a letting go, a giving up, and rebirth is an implicit part of this process. So a dream of death portends a possible change. A baby in a dream implies that a birth is coming into being in one's mind, or it may represent immature parts of oneself according to the context.

Like some plays, some dreams have a setting, a plot, and a message behind these. According to the way the components of a dream are related, each person's situation, attitudes, reactions, and emotional states are displayed in the dream. The timeless quality of dreams has already been mentioned. If one always looks for a statement of the past, and present situations, and a hint of what future actions are required, these aspects will always be found in a dream. Sometimes dreams foretell the future.

A man dreamt that he was sitting in an office overlooking Plymouth Sound, when a small black cloud formed low over the inner harbour. From it came flashes of lighting. This was a strange happening, for the scene was commonplace and the day fine. The meaning was not understood, nor at the time was the recorder aware of the extent of dream symbolism, and he did not then believe that future events were found in dreams. Though he had heard of J. W. Dunne, he had not read his books. A few days later he experienced an unusually severe outburst of temper over a trivial matter sitting in exactly the same situation, looking at the same scene he had seen in the dream. Its meaning then dawned on him. After that he paid a good deal of attention to his dreams, and learnt a lot about himself with their help. Years later he was looking up the significance of another dream symbol in a book by C. J. Jung, and read that a thunderstorm also has the meaning of a fertilizing act. On reflecting he realized that the episode had been a fertilizing act. That experience had given him the energy to go deeply into his inner world with far-reaching results to his life.

Not all dreams are so fruitful; some imply that the dreamer may die. There are the classical two described by Jung of an ardent mountaineer who, exhilarated in a dream, jumped out into space. He fell to his death shortly after. A girl dreamt of a horse jumping out of a window to its death far below. Her symptoms of weakness, thought at first to be psychological, were those of a fatal wasting of the muscles. A woman, responding to psychotherapy, had repeated dreams of swimming against the current and slipping away from her doctor who was holding out a helping hand. Thorough investigations showed no abnormalities, but when an exploratory operation was done, her cancer was too far advanced for treatment. Dreams of animals attacking the dreamer usually mean illnesses, the severity and outcome are indicated by the size of the animal, the savagery and success of the attack.

Dreams do not pull their punches and all big ones are worth pondering over deeply. Anyone who is sceptical is recommended to record his dreams over a few months. If the information given here on dream interpretation is used, the effort will be found worth while. Reading one's dreams years later makes a lot of sense of events one didn't understand at the time, and sometimes still provides a basis for future actions. This advice is given because a lot of useful information is lost when people think it is only a dream, and do not bother to pay attention to it.

Besides dreams which everyone has, some people have visions. These are not rare if day-dreaming is counted. Fairly frequent also are the people who see someone they are attached to at the time of death. It is so common that there is no need to give examples. This may occur in a dream or as a waking vision. Such visions are no more than a slight temporary decreasc in the filtering action of the brain which prevents us from getting these sort of impressions all the time. They are induced by the intensity of the relationship between the two people concerned, which is being broken. This statement begs a lot of questions, but implies that emotions are a real force. They are. They affect the mind and body. However, there is no need to get excited about this. It is normal. But many people do get excited if they have a vision. They can think they are going mad. Or, if they do not think so, their relations or doctors may do so. A young girl lived in a village, known for its higher than average emotional instability. When her grandfather died she had a vision of him shortly afterwards. She was terrified, and told her mother, who was horrified and called the doctor. There was so much excitement, she became uncontrollable and was popped into the local asylum. She steadied up after three weeks and came out labelled as having had a schizophrenic interlude. She remained shy and withdrawn, believing herself to be potentially mad. After it was explained to her that what she had had was a common, normal experience, that it might happen again when another close relative died, and that she was in no way mad, she cheered up considerably. In fact, it was her fears of insanity that had made her so upset.

People who see visions often, who can perceive details about another person from contact with them either by sight, hearing, an inner voice, or perception are more common than is generally realized. They are often frightened by their unwanted abilities, and suppress them as much as possible. They don't talk about them because other people get frightened, hostile, or sceptical, and they would much rather not have them. However, some people exploit these abilities for power, or gain, or excitement, and are imitated by impostors.

The ability to water divine is another human faculty that is even more common. Most people can do it to a certain extent if they practice. Not only water can be divined, so can metals and people. Some people can also dowse from a map, others can use this faculty to answer questions, the answers to which they cannot know. But this faculty is not a party game, and sceptical enquirers usually get wrong answers which only confirm their normal emotional states. The mind must be open, and its state balanced and accepting, otherwise these extra-sensory perceptions do not penetrate the conscious mind.

There are other odd human phenomena which do not fit into the laws of physical chemistry—ghosts and poltergeists, for instance. They can, like the other sorts of experience just mentioned, be observed by only a minority, and not at will even by these. So they cannot be proved by the scientific method. But this does not mean they are not real and law-abiding. It is just that the laws are not the same as those of physics and chemistry. There is no need to get excited when odd psychic phenomena occur, not even enough to deny their existence. It is only by being calm, open, and receptive that a person can learn. This is the state that one gets into by doing the watch exercise. By denying the truth of anything which another person asserts, you are doing violence to yourself, and the other.

Your mind is using its productive function to prevent its filtering function being acknowledged. The outer personality is defending its existence, which depends on not admitting the possibility of the existence of another mode of consciousness. The emotional content is one of self-love, and only other disturbed emotional reactions occur—denial, negative thinking, rejection and violence. This is the way the personality defends itself against penetration by views which it cannot reconcile with its existence. So always approach anything in the watch state, ready to reconcile and incorporate anything new. If this is not done, neither change nor growth is possible. Being ready to receive is the only way.

8
A Human Being's Possibilities

SOME people have to learn the lesson from life that you can't win all the time, and others that there are times when you must win, and this doesn't mean that occasionally you will be lucky. It is inevitable that sometimes absolute inflexibility of will, intention, and force must be exerted. No examples can be given of the situations when either course should be followed. They will be different for everyone. To give an example might make someone do the wrong thing when it was important. There can be nothing theoretical about the situations when the type of action being discussed here takes place. Each one requires an immediate and practical response. It is no good saying that in all circumstances I will do good. There may be occasions when this is impossible. Nevertheless, the only thing that is definite is that more people have to learn to give in and accept, than those who have to learn the opposite. This is because the personality is based on the productive function of the brain, which affects the mind, so that the predominant emotion is self-love. This is enhanced by the brain's filtering action which prevents other perceptions entering consciousness, to contradict the personality. Thinking, and feeling based only on previously established facts, form the apparent proof to the individual that this is how it ought to be with him. The built in 'I'm all right, Jack' nature of the human being's personality is a fantastic thing. It allows him to poison his environment, while admiring himself for putting men on a dead moon; to preach universal brotherhood based on slave labour, and all the other oddities of the previous chapters. The real trouble is that he believes his personality—this mixed up thing—is himself. It is not. The problem now is—how can a personality become a human being? Well the first thing is to realize that you are in a mess, and to try and do something about it. If you can't see that, you are in a jam. There is no chance of changing yourself. You are satisfied with yourself and will stay as you are.

But, if you want to change, you can start looking into your personality—don't be frightened or disgusted—it isn't your fault. But, if you don't take the opportunity to change, it will be your responsibility for staying as you are.

The watch exercise is only one of many ways of starting to put the personality in order, by getting beyond it, or inside it, or of becoming childlike again, and starting to grow. One has to go back to a state of mind in which one can learn in order to grow mentally.

When in the degree of attention induced by the watch exercise, it is possible to understand that one can do nothing without an aim, or intention. One also has a consciousness which takes in the sense of being oneself, of existing, thinking, feeling, and of sense impressions from the body and surroundings. Nothing will happen, unless one wants to do it sufficiently to make the necessary effort. So there have to be three things going on in the mind before anything can change in it—Aim, Consciousness and Will. Consider giving up smoking—unless one has the intention—that is, makes an aim to do so, one never will. Unless one is aware enough to be conscious of when one is smoking, as well as remembering the aim not to, there is no chance of doing so. Finally, unless one wants to stop enough to make a real effort, even if the other two components are present, one gives up the effort because the will is lacking. These parts of oneself are quite close to the sense of I—of being me—that one has. They belong to the part that observes what is going on, and registers various types of impressions, both mental (thoughts and feelings), and from the senses. This exercise demonstrates that the part that observes and says I, need not be the thoughts, feelings, or the sense impressions. But it takes a lot of energy to maintain the watching state. Most of the day is spent responding automatically to habits of mind, and the situation one is in. As long as one is comfortable and has no problems, or is not challenged by anyone else, one drifts along in a state of no attention at the mercy of one's environment and habits of mind. There is actually no awareness of what is going on, and one is dependent entirely upon the skills that have been learnt, past imprintings and associations, and the reactions upon them of the events in one's surroundings, If one is challenged by being asked what is one doing, one wakes up quickly, thinks out an answer, and gives that as the reason. It can be correct, but may be completely misleading, if a response to an unknown—that is subconscious—habit or association was producing one's response. For instance, one may be arranging, without any particular feelings, about the best site for a picnic, when a dog passes by. Now, in childhood, a dog may have attacked one. Unconsciously old fears are aroused, coupled maybe with aggressive feelings towards dogs. The peaceful discussion changes into a surprisingly fierce argument. Then, if asked why the quarrel, the answer will be that the other person was being stupid. But there does not have to be a challenge in order to start thinking and feeling consciously about a situation. If one becomes uncomfortable, or a problem develops, one starts to do this. Previously reactions have been absolutely automatic without any real responsibility at all. Now a solution to the problem can be worked out, or the discomfort removed. There can be an extensive change in behaviour—but only in response to the event, and one's previously established habits of mind. For instance, you can decide to marry or not, wear this or that piece of clothing, go to the cinema, take your asthma to a doctor, go to the moon, stand on your head, but you still have all your problems, and perhaps a few more. At this level of attention it is impossible to change the habits of mind, but considerable alterations in behaviour can result from avoiding, suppressing and compensating for them.

It is only when the watch exercise state of attention is present, that one learns anything, or can change a habit. Otherwise nothing new comes in. There is only reaction to events, which themselves may be new, but in the old way. There may be an apparent change because the event reacted to is new, but the response was already determined by what is already in existence. So there can be no change in the human being who is responding to the event.

The diagram below sums up what the watch exercise shows.

		Some attention
Sense of 'I'	Aim—intention Consciousness—awareness Will—wanting—value	Can change both habits of mind and behaviour—can make new aims—can form new habits.
	OBSERVES ↓ (WATCHES)	
		Little attention
	Thinking Feeling	Cannot change habits of mind. Can change behaviour extensively, but only in response to demands or events and the old habits of mind.

No attention

The human animal maintains its existence by responding automatically to: Sense impressions Appetites (Drives) —hunger —territorial —inertia —sex —exploration —contact Knowledge (Memory) Imagination (Fantasy)	Can change neither habits of mind nor behaviour. Nothing new enters. At the mercy of life, since reactions are wholly governed by associations.

In using the watch exercise to change troublesome old reactions, the easy way is not to pry deep into the reasons why these habits occur, but to make an aim to change the habit, and use the watch state to substitute a new form of behaviour. In other words, an aim is made to behave in a different way. A good all-purpose aim is to give the situation what it needs. Refuse to respond in your habitual way. Look at the situation with a detached adult eye, and give it, or the other person involved, what is needed. It may be necessary to say 'no', or to give in. An acceptance of the appropriate reaction is required. To do otherwise is to enter a state of disturbed emotions which burst out, or smoulder on, and produce the various disorders described in Chapters 5 and 6. If you want to go further and work on a deeper level—or higher you could say—it doesn't matter which, the middle level of the watch exercise diagram is being considered now—decide which is your main disturbed emotion. All the emotions are very fluid. They rapidly change one into the other whether they are disturbed or not. But since there are more disturbed emotions, the variations of the attitudes resulting from them are enormous. The main human attitudes are listed in Chapter 5, and summarized on the chart at the end of it. Most people have more than one emotional disturbance. But pick one to work on at a time. It is easier. Then find out what situations produce the disturbance. It is useful to keep a written record of these situations. For example, you may have a difficulty in facing older people, or more senior people, and asserting your own point of view. There may be a difficulty in living with a person of the opposite sex—you may like your own way too much, and find the natural resistance of others irritating.

Suppose the problem is fear, and symptoms of anxiety are troublesome. There is fatigue, palpitations, tremulous feelings, cold feet and hands, nervous tension and so on. Such people worry about everything. There are two types of worry. Not doing what has to be done and falling behind, and then getting fearful of the consequences; or, starting to get frightened of dealing with a future event before one has to, and then assuming that the worst is going to happen. Decide which group you belong to—the second is more common in habitual worriers with anxiety states—and start recording examples of your favourite worries. In women it is usually an accident to the children or husband. In men it may be making a mistake, losing their job, or becoming impotent. Then, alerted by these observations, start lifting the pick-up each time you find yourself playing over one of your favourite worry theme songs. Use the watch exercise to check the state of worry and substitute a new, useful response. If you can't check the state this way, go out of doors and take a few deep breaths—break it up somehow. Do something silly, like hopping on one leg.

If your problem is depression, study your depressive habits of mind. You will find that a common one is the haunting assumption that whatever you are engaged in is going to go wrong on you; that what you are doing isn't worth while, or has no meaning. The trouble is that for the occupation in itself, or for your life itself, this is so often true. Some jobs and some ways of living are dull, monotonous, and meaningless. That is why depression can get such a hold on a person. But the use of life to an individual, apart from developing a 'beautiful, successful personality,' and being rich and happy ever afterwards, and other such idiocies, is to let him grow as a human being. So it is well worth while spending a little time and effort.

If these observations are not jotted down when they are perceived, the suppressive self-love of the personality soon sees they are forgotten. So get into the habit of making a note as soon as something is seen, and take the opportunity to ponder over it later. Soon a number of situations will be known, in which an attempt can be made to transform the emotional response, into its positive tolerant form. The greatest difficulty in doing this lies in the redirection of the excessive emotions to the right degree. People trapped in states of too much faith, hope, and charity find it difficult to understand that their intensity of feeling produces the same state of imbalance as the negative types of emotion, which so clearly seem wrong to them.

There is not only the need to transform disturbed negative emotions into tranquil positive ones, but also to balance the relative intensities with which faith, hope and charity are experienced. Having an aim, remembered as often as possible, to bring equal intensities of the three primary emotions into all actions, knowing what they are, and asking oneself if they are present equally in everything one does, produces tranquillity of mind and body, as well as satisfactory results.

Because of the nature of the world, and the way in which the personality is formed, we have in us strong tendencies to experience disturbed emotions as well as a desire to be peaceful and tranquil. To live we have to destroy. Every animal kills to eat—we have to—otherwise we die. Even vegetables have to be killed—even if they are eaten raw, our teeth tear them to pieces and our stomachs digest them. Maybe killing animals in order to eat is a little more disturbing—we are animals too—but a lot of false sentiment is expanded on abhorring cannibalism, and by vegetarians on not eating animals, though there is nothing that can be said in favour of killing for pleasure, except by those who enjoy violence. We all have to accept the inescapable necessity of killing to live. So we have to balance the inescapable need to destroy—violence—with the need to be peaceful and tolerant.

To live on earth is to be in an unavoidable, unstable state of tension, of balancing good and evil, right and wrong. It is not possible to avoid this, unless one opts out of being human, and becomes an automaton. Unfortunately this is common. But if one wants to try being human, not just a machine, or an animal, life becomes an interesting struggle to evolve. Instead of accepting the fact that the brain and the body degenerate with age, and giving up, or fighting to maintain the personality in the state to which it is accustomed, every moment has the possibility of learning something new about oneself, and altering one's old reactions, of integrating the animal and human sides, and the conscious with the unconscious. One becomes a tube through which life flows. One remains young for the fountain is always overflowing.

But is this all there is to life? Is it only a happy, contented, self-study as one ages? Well, of course not—but it is as far as doing the watch exercise and work on your personality will get you—farther than necessary a good many will say, and there can be no denying that the great majority of people only wish to do the minimum of self-enquiry. So, if this is your opinion, stop here—the book ended at the last paragraph. But, for those who feel that there is more to existence than right living it might be worth going on to the end.

What states of attention exist beyond that produced by doing the watch exercise? It is difficult to discuss the field of human experience now being considered. It is not readily reproducible, is highly personal, and only comes to people transiently, most often during sexual orgasm. If you are not aware of its existence, and able to discriminate it from the normal state of consciousness, its significance will be missed, and it will be accepted as a normal part of the experience associated with it—which is usual with sexual orgasm. It is an extraordinary and very satisfactory experience. That is why sex is so valued. But let us see what this experience is in itself—free from the heavy instinctive overtones of sex. A lad of nine was walking alone on a large farm when he came on two dogs attacking a sow and her sucklings. The sow was hard put to it, for the dogs were after a meal of juicy young pork, and she had about seven to protect. The boy beat the dogs off with a stick, but the sow, blind with rage, went for him, and started to bite his knee. This was a terrible surprise. He was feeling very pleased with himself and had thought that the sow would be grateful. Suddenly, in his panic, as she seemed much bigger than he, and everything seemed to be going wrong, he knew what to do. Everything slowed up and became sharp and clear. He shortened his hold on the stick and rammed its broken end up her snout. At the same time he bent his knee up so that the skin tightened and she lost her grip on his knee-cap. He rolled over, hopped free and gave her a good belt with the stick. It took only two seconds to happen, but it seemed infinitely slow, easy and powerful. There was absolute confidence in the outcome. The sow turned aside and went back to her farrow. The sun was bright and hot. There were only a few tooth marks on his knee, which did not hurt much. Then things went back to normal speed. Another example was of a man teaching a friend to drive. In Germany just after the war they were going down a one-way lane on the right, and were crossing a bridge over a high cutting, when a lorry suddenly turned off the oncoming lane into their path, doing a U turn. Instead of running out to the right, the learner forgot he was on the Continent, and went left. There was no room to pass the lorry that way, so he went harder over and headed for the low parapet and a drop of about 80 feet. He suddenly gave up and said, 'Help, what shall I do?' Again there was that sudden change of speed and instant clarity of mind and sensation.

The other man struck the driver's hands off the wheel—span it the opposite way so that they hit the barrier a glancing blow, and then went on spinning it so that they skidded round in a circle and stopped. For the driver had by this time got going with the brakes. Very little damage was done except that the front wheel was bent. The lorry never stopped. Then things slowed down again and the teacher began to feel frightened when he looked at the drop they had escaped from.

The common characteristic of these two episodes of change in consciousness, is that they both have a sudden emergency, and an element of danger. There is a choiceless awareness of there being only one thing to do. There is an apparent slowing up of time, so that there seems to be ample time to do actions which must have taken place very quickly. In other words the speed of perception of time is vastly increased. Such an event is never forgotten. There is also an access of power. To turn a four-wheel drive command car at 60 m.p.h., requires a lot of force from the passenger's seat. The increase of bodily power, and another feature of this state are illustrated in the next example. An undergraduate was rowing in Trial eights trying to make an impression on the selectors. He was in the weaker crew, and so at a disadvantage. A beaten crew never rows as well, or tries as hard as possible. The people who know that they have not got a chance of being finally chosen give up. This makes it harder work for those who want to be selected. Knowing all this, the young man determined to row every stroke with all his power. After one-third of the race his crew were well behind and he felt at the end of his resources, but kept on. Suddenly he was free of his labouring body's distress. He was still aware of it, but was also outside it. The effort was gone. There was the usual feeling of having all the time in the world. He could watch his performance, as if he were a coach, and keep it as neat as possible. This state was sustained until the end of the race, but there was not much interest in it. His crew slipped farther and farther behind. At the finish his consciousness went back into the body as it recovered. The new feature here, apart from the sustaining of the state for about ten minutes, is the feeling of being outside the body. This is described in various books on Indian Yoga and in *The Secret of the Golden Flower* translated from the Chinese. Dr. Roger Bannister also describes this state which he experienced when running the first four-minute mile. Dr. W. Sargent gives numerous examples in his book *Battle for the Mind.* This phenomenon must be experienced quite often by long distance athletes, but as it is a very successful experience to have, once you know how to do it, athletics being a competitive activity, you keep quiet. Perhaps that is why it is not heard of much. The ingredients for producing the experience are: willingly accepting extreme physical exhaustion, and a joyous intention to carry out that activity to the utmost of one's power. At the same time there must be an aim to enter the state that is being described. Such is the degree of physical power which the body can be willed to exert in this state that a warning is necessary. Do not try to enter the state by this means unless you are young, fully fit physically, and have nothing wrong with your heart. It is an exhilarating experience, and in the excitement of experiencing it you may tear a muscle or ligament severely, or even kill yourself if, for instance, you have coronary artery disease—as practically everyone over fifty has.

So far the examples given have all been associated with danger, severe physical exertion, sexual orgasm or meditation. Another, also physical, activity, which brings the experience, is when a woman is consciously willing the act of childbirth. The mescaline and lysergic acid group of drugs also produces a similar result, when a person isn't too excited or frightened by its other effects, and is in a positive emotional state. Aim is always important. The physical aspects of the examples so far given have conditioned the response of the mind to the new state of consciousness. In more peaceable circumstances it may be entered spontaneously as described by Dr. Bucke in *Cosmic Consciousness*, and called samadhi by the Hindus and Buddhists, satori by the Zen Buddhists, and whatever their current name for it is, by the Sufis. All these ways of reaching a higher degree of consciousness —especially the last two—require working with other people in a systematic way. Working in a group tends to produce a group personality. Rules are needed to keep order. There has to be a teacher, and as the group grows a hierarchy has to form. Group attitudes develop. All this is inevitable, but imposes a distortion on the people who are attracted by the group's aims. Self-love soon takes over and develops an organization in which the original aim—to be selfless, and let a new conscious state enter if it will—is lost. This difficulty is well recognized by the Sufis, and many others who have been great teachers. The historical proof of this statement is so clear in the development of the Christian Church, that it is not necessary to labour the point further. Probably the Sufis have stood the test of time better than any other, but they are still an organization. So its members, who may need help in order to mature, and weaken their personalities, will have to suffer the price of belonging to an organization.

Eventually an individual who is interested in further growth may realize that there must be freedom from the influence of organizations. This does not mean that he must not belong to an organization, or cease to cooperate in the activities of his community. However much he has to take part because of his position, he will do so willingly, but without a sense of personal involvement. When this realization has been made, many previous ambitions, and activities, may seem meaningless. Some will inevitably be dropped, for the individual will then see that the time previously occupied by them can be better spent. The adjustments in the outer life that then take place may seem pointless, or even strange, to friends and colleagues, but this is inevitable.

Once it has been possible to separate from the rigid mechanical aspects of outer life, there is more time and energy—more mental room—for personal relationships which become wider and deeper, but may also change for the same reasons as the relationship with the organizations. There is no sitting back and taking it easy. Work, mental and physical, is the essential basis of life. Idleness is stagnation, a denial of universal change. Stagnation leads to decay, and decay to death. It is impossible to escape from the necessity of submitting to universal laws. The meaning of acceptance of life on earth is now clearer. Living becomes holding a state of emotional consciousness while trying to give every moment its appropriate reaction; balancing the three positive emotions, so that one can be open to experience that state, which is so free there is no choice. It is a paradox that in lower degrees of attention there is a wider choice of action, but less free will. With greater attention, and more understanding there is no choice, but abounding free will. Free will is Love. In a state of choiceless awareness, there is Love. It has to be experienced. It cannot be described. What is commonly called love is, at its best, what has been called charity in this book, and at its worst, self-love. These are not Love. To be able to experience Love one must be ready to receive it. But it will only come to one as a gift. This experience contains the meaning of Life. The right aim of living is to exist in order to enter the consciousness of Love.

INDEX